Upper-class English in Natural and Audiovisual Dialogue

ŁÓDŹ STUDIES IN LANGUAGE

Edited by Barbara Lewandowska-Tomaszczyk and Łukasz Bogucki

VOLUME 69

PETER LANG

Luca Valleriani

Upper-class English in Natural and Audiovisual Dialogue

PETER LANG

**Bibliographic Information published by the
Deutsche Nationalbibliothek**
The Deutsche Nationalbibliothek lists this publication in the Deutsche
Nationalbibliografie; detailed bibliographic data is available online at
http://dnb.d-nb.de.

Library of Congress Cataloging-in-Publication Data
A CIP catalog record for this book has been applied for
at the Library of Congress.

Cover illustration: Courtesy of Benjamin Ben Chaim.

This publication was financially supported by the Department of European,
American and Intercultural Studies at the Sapienza University of Rome.

ISSN 1437-5281
ISBN 978-3-631-86296-4 (Print)
E-ISBN 978-3-631-86298-8 (E-PDF)
E-ISBN 978-3-631-86338-1 (EPUB)
DOI 10.3726/b18768

© Peter Lang GmbH
Internationaler Verlag der Wissenschaften
Berlin 2021
All rights reserved.

Peter Lang – Berlin · Bern · Bruxelles · New York ·
Oxford · Warszawa · Wien

This publication has been peer reviewed.

www.peterlang.com

I think there could be nothing more hopelessly non-U than to write a book about it.

(Russel Lynes, introduction to *Noblesse Oblige,* edited by Nancy Mitford, 1959)

Acknowledgements

Many people helped me, directly or indirectly, during the years of my doctoral studies. In particular, I would like to thank:

First of all, my supervisor, Professor Irene Ranzato, for being an inspiring mentor and an encouraging and caring advisor. Without her guidance and support, this volume would not have come to light. I am also grateful to her for finding an academic potential in me and for involving me in new opportunities and challenges, thus contributing to my professional and personal development.

All the other English lecturers at the Department of European, American and Intercultural Studies at Sapienza University for showing interest in my research and for often providing helpful advice.

My Ph.D. colleagues, with whom I can always share my doubts and experiences.

All the researchers that I have met during conferences and seminars, who provided cues to explore new directions.

My friends and family, for offering me enjoyable social-life moments that recharged my mental energy.

Table of contents

List of tables and waveforms

Introduction

As author Evelyn Waugh wrote in a letter to his friend Nancy Mitford, "in England class distinctions have always roused higher feelings than national honour" (1959, 93), and spoken language is one of the main elements that people generally judge to make assumptions about the social background of a speaker. Upper-class English, in particular, is a recognisable language variety in Britain, spoken by the aristocracy and the descendants of the landed gentry. This variety, which is generally associated to a specific upper-class accent, has recently been used in more than one case in telecinematic dialogue to provide a realistic portrayal of the members of the high society in the UK. This study, which originated from my doctoral thesis, will deal with the description of modern upper-class English in natural face-to-face situations and how it is rendered in the fictional audiovisual dialogue.

Although members of the élite are easily recognisable for the way they speak, the language of the British upper classes is to be considered a rather under-researched topic. Scholars of English sociolinguistics have always focused more on the language of the lower classes, both in their linguistic history and features, as well as their translation into other languages. Upper classes, on the contrary, have not been explored as much and it is not difficult to find out the reasons why not many scholars investigated them. First of all, studying the language of a social class is never an easy task, simply because it is difficult to define the concept of social class itself even from the sociological point of view, due to aspects like heterogeneity and social mobility (Trudgill 2000, 26); in other words, society is fluid, social classes are aggregates of similar but not identical individuals, and they can easily move up or down the social hierarchy (ibid.). Secondly, the upper strata of any society are usually characterised by a form of insularity and exclusivity which makes it very complicated for researchers to penetrate even for study purposes (Kroch 1996, 26–27; Ranzato 2017, 27 and 2018, 204).

Before delving into the discussion regarding the objectives and research questions of this project, some space should be devoted to the introduction and explanation of the topic through some basic sociolinguistic concepts. In particular, while this study is to be considered as part of the wide research field of dialectology and language variation, it focuses on a particular kind of language variety called 'sociolect.' Peter Trudgill defines a sociolect as "a variety or lect which is thought of as being related to its speakers' social background rather than geographical background" (2003, 122) and, exactly as it happens with regional dialects whose boundaries often coincide with geographical barriers, sociolinguistic variation can also be explained in terms of social barriers, such as age, gender, religion, ethnicity or social class (2000, 24). To use Eugen Coseriu's terms (1969, 149, expanding from Flydal 1952), a sociolect is a variety of language that is placed along the diastratic axis of the architecture of language, and it is to be distinguished from both the diatopic (geolect/dialect) and the diaphasic conceptualisations (styles and registers); most of the studies in language variation are grounded on this model, which has been discussed and reconceptualised by several scholars, such as Lieb 1993, Berruto 2003, Hernández-Campoy 2016, among others.

The distinction between diastratic and diaphasic variation is particularly relevant, because 'upper-class speech' is sometimes identified as a style (Kroch 1996, 39), while it will be argued in this research that it is a recognisable and defined linguistic code in the United Kingdom, characterised by specific linguistic features, especially from the phonological point of view, which are shared by the members of the high society. In this book it will be illustrated that, more than in the cases of other social-class dialects, the upper classes could arguably be considered as a form of speech community in the Labovian sense (1972), "a locus in which speakers agree on the social meanings and evaluation of the variants used" (Milroy and Milroy 1997, 51), but also that the level of consciousness of the variability in language use does not imply that upper-class speech is a mere formal or 'heightened' style. As it happens with any other language variety, the upper-class speaker can choose to emphasise some linguistic features according to the context, but his/her every-day neutral speech is also to be considered as an upper-class speech because it contains specific lexical features and phonological phenomena, as it will be further explored in the course of the chapters.

The fact that the upper-class speech in the UK has a phonemic specificity is an important factor because it means that this sociolect has a corresponding accent, which can be identified as a conservative variant of the Received Pronunciation, defined by John C. Wells as U-RP (1992, 279).

This accent is highly recognisable and it is, as argued by Ranzato, "the base of the stereotyped or at least old-fashioned rendition of the members of this class in cinematographic films and television series." (2018, 205). Audiovisual texts are a fundamental tool to explore the sociolect of the upper British society, which gives a great opportunity to study at least the representation of this dialect.

This first section served as a presentation of the topic of this study, which intends to explore the language of the British upper-classes in all linguistic aspects through the comparison between the natural dialogue and the represented telecinematic dialogue. Therefore, this project belongs primarily to the wide research areas of sociolinguistics and dialectology, but it will also deal with issues related to other fields like the analysis of audiovisual dialogue, the history of the English language and, to some extent, audiovisual translation.

I. What is upper class?

The exact definition of the British upper class from a sociological perspective is problematic.[1] In fact, it has always been difficult to conduct scientific and statistical studies within the high society, whose 'borders' with the upper-middle and middle social stratifications are often arbitrarily traced by its members, as Anthony Kroch (1996) also argues referring to the upper class in Philadelphia:

> Unlike classes defined by sociologists or sociolinguists on the basis of statistical indices, the upper class is a self-recognized group whose members frequently meet face-to-face in social institutions of their own. The group is extremely self-conscious and demarcates itself sharply from the middle-class. [...]. Financially, the upper class is based on inherited wealth. (ibid., 25).

Even though Kroch's study was carried out in an American context, his definition of the upper class can be applied to the British area, too, especially at the time of his research, when the most authoritative measure of social class in the UK was still the Nuffield class schema; this measuring

---

1   See Block (2014) for a complete discussion on the problem of defining the general concept of social class and how it was adopted historically in Applied Linguistics.

system was codified in 1970 in the National Statistics Socio-Economic Classification and its main objective was that of categorising people into different social groups according to their occupations. This first model, despite a few updates in the following decade, did not take into consideration social and cultural aspects that, on the contrary, might play a defining role in the processes of class divisions (Rose and Pevalin 2003). Just to give an example, the social group at the top of the hierarchy was that of the "Higher managerial and professional occupations," which is not a clear indication for the socio-cultural background of the members of the group, making it, most probably, highly heterogeneous from the linguistic point of view. Occupation and education, however, as it will also be discussed in the first chapter, are not enough to define social-class belonging.

It was with the aim of incorporating other dimensions that a group of sociologists elaborated a new model of social class distinction a few years ago. This model was used for the BBC's 2011 Great British Class Survey (GBCS), which is considered to be the largest survey of social class ever conducted in the UK (Savage et al. 2013). The GBCS demonstrated "the existence of an 'elite,' whose wealth separates them from an established middle class, as well as a class of technical experts and a class of 'new affluent' workers" (ibid, 220). Such results were the consequence of an attentive analysis which took into consideration three different aspects, namely the social, the cultural and the economic capital. A map of seven classes was proposed after the collecting of data and at the top of this map there is a social group called 'class 1: Elite.'

The group of the 'elite' can be identified as that of the British upper class and, following the GBCS description (ibid, 233–234), it is characterised by:

• the highest levels of every form of capital (especially the economic one, since their mean household income almost doubles that of the next highest class);
• the lowest proportion of ethnic minorities;
• the highest proportion of graduates;
• a geographical concentration of their residences in the South East of England, especially in the areas close to London in the affluent Home Counties.

To put it short, the definition of the 'elite' is that of "a relatively small, socially and spatially exclusive group at the apex of British society, whose economic wealth sets them apart from the great majority of the population" (ibid).

Therefore, what is intended as 'upper class' in this research is the most advantaged and privileged social group in the UK, which is indicated as the 'elite' by the above-mentioned authoritative sociological research. In particular, I find – together with Kroch (1996, 25) and Ranzato (2018, 204) – the aspect of the inherited wealth as the most relevant one. In fact, this research has particularly focused on the study of the language of what we can call, maybe anachronistically, the British aristocracy, whose purpose in life "is most emphatically not to work for money." (Mitford 1959, 33). Therefore, this research will deal with the language of the British aristocracy specifically and not with that of the upper-middle class.

II. Literature review

Before Kroch (1996) – who, however, did not focus on the British area, but carried out a study on the upper-class speech in Philadelphia, and whose result was that the only significant distinctions were on the prosodic and lexical level (ibid., 25) – the language of the upper-class people in Britain had been the focus of what Ranzato defines as the "U/non-U debate of the late 1950s" (2018, 205), using the acronym coined by Alan Ross in a ground-breaking albeit old-fashioned and partly impressionistic article (1954). Naturally, class distinction through language had already raised some interest even before that date, but just as "the subject of feverish but very private debate," (Waugh 1959, 93). A re-edited version of Ross's article was included in a volume edited by Mitford herself in 1959 where she collected a few writings about the English aristocracy. As it can be read in the volume, Waugh was not the only one who felt the debate on the upper-class speech as being scarcely interesting; in fact, Peter Fleming also wrote that such interest was "unhealthy and contrary to the national interest," although he also admitted that the 'U' speech "is not – as many believe – an arrogant and 'snooty' institution, used mainly [...] for outfacing non-U speakers. It is the natural idiom of a comparatively small class and exists to further the purpose of communication within that class." (1959, 127–128).

As mentioned above, although his study is rooted on anecdotal evidence more than concrete data, Ross was the first one to provide a list of features both in written and spoken English that were to be considered, in his own opinion and experience, either as 'U' ("to designate usages of the upper class" 1959, 11) or 'non-U' ("to designate usages which are not upper class" ibid.). It is true that, contrarily to the other authors who contributed to Mitford's *Noblesse Oblige*, who were mostly novelists or journalists, Ross was a scholar and a linguist, but he compiled his list largely basing on his personal experience, being an upper-class member himself,[2] and on Mitford's novels, especially *The Pursuit of Love* (1945), as it will be discussed in Chapter 1.

Not only was Ross-Mitford's terminological dichotomy embraced by prominent people of their period, but it is also sometimes still adopted in scholarly works (Wales 1994, Mesthrie et al. 2009, Gregory 2008, Warde 2011, Ranzato 2017 and 2018, among others), suggesting a scarce scholarly interest in the topic in the field of descriptive sociolinguistics, whose most renowned studies have as their upper limit the 'upper middle class' (Mesthrie *et al.* 2009, 100). Even a prominent figure like Peter Trudgill did not analyse the upper class in his Labovian research on the language of people of Norwich (ibid.). Therefore, for this reason, but also because the literature on the 'U/non-U debate' is to be considered, as already mentioned, as the basis of the stereotypical construction of the aristocratic characters' language in films and TV series (Ranzato 2018, 205), this research will also refer to Ross's essays, especially in the section regarding the upper-class lexical features, which is the aspect that raised most of the controversies in the 1950s. It will also be taken into consideration that Ross's argumentation has even been revisited and expanded during the last few decades in mainstream non-fiction books that contain as many fascinatingly detailed linguistic indications, despite not being grounded on a scientific method (Buckle 1978; Fox 2004; Taggart 2010).

*

---

2   He was defined by Russel Lynes as "a U scholar in a non-U university," referring to the University of Birmingham (1959, x).

In the field of English sociolinguistics, upper-class speech has traditionally been identified with Received Pronunciation (RP), whose label was originally conceived to indicate the standard accent and soon became associated with the people of high society. However, nowadays linguists generally agree on the fact that "no accent is a homogeneous invariant monolith – certainly not RP. So we must [...] consider the variability found in it" (Wells 1992, 279). In particular, Wells identified a conservative version of RP, generally spoken by the Royal Family, the High Courts and most of the members of Parliament, as opposed to the so-called Mainstream RP. This 'upper' version is defined by Wells as Upper-crust RP (or U-RP) and its main features will be listed in the first chapter of this volume. As it will be discussed, some scholars (Gimson 1984; Ramsaran 1990; Cruttenden 2014) have proposed alternative names for this accent, but after Wells (1992) there have been no updated taxonomies on the upper-class variety in Britain, apart from sparse insights on those linguistic features that can be defined, following Mugglestone, as symbols of social divide (2007). Mugglestone, however, dealt more with the concept of 'educatedness' rather than social-class issues, stating that "the 'cultivated speaker' employs a definite number of sounds which he utters with precision, distinctness, and in their proper places" (ibid., 53), but given that the level of education can be somehow related to social class, citations from her research will be included in this work too. Wales's article (1994) on what she defines as 'Royalese' will also be cited as a main reference in the brief section devoted to the morpho-syntactic description of upper-class English.

Despite the fact that there are no recent academic investigations on upper-class English, a few scholars have recently acknowledged the existence of a gap in the sociolinguistic field; Trudgill (2008), Britain (2017) and Fabricius (2018), in particular, have observed that the standard language and the élite sociolect have been identified as a unique identity for too long, so that, as a consequence, upper-class speakers have rarely been the subject of particularised studies. This research will thus try to demonstrate that "the connection between standard dialects and elite dialects is not straightforward." (Britain 2017, 289).

The only recent contribution which deals specifically with upper-class English is Ranzato's discussion on the phonological and sociocultural aspects of the upper strata in British society and the various functions played by upper-class characters in different films and TV series (2018). This work is an insightful expansion of what the same author wrote in the RP-dedicated section of her book on the accents of England, where she explores U-RP as a well-defined and recognisable point in the accent continuum (2017, 27–39). As mentioned above, Ranzato also examined the representations and functions of the upper-class accent in telecinematic dialogue, where the British aristocrat is a recurrent trope. It is not by chance, in fact, that the topic of the upper-class speech has recently been the focus of research within the audiovisual translation field, with studies dealing with the translation strategies adopted to render the language of this speech community in the target language, which apparently tend to draw on lexical and prosodic expedients to compensate for the loss of the phonological peculiarities (Bruti and Vignozzi 2016; Sandrelli 2016).

III. Objectives and methodology[3]

Given the lack of a complete modern study on the English language as spoken by the British upper classes, one of the aims of this volume will be that of reorganising the sparse information on the topic that is found in the linguistic and sociocultural studies that were mentioned in the previous section. While doing so, these bibliographical contents, which, in some cases, need updating, will be discussed and expanded in the light of new evidence and through an attempt to verify when a linguistic feature can be considered as an indicator or marker of the upper-class sociolect or rather as a stereotypical characteristic, to use the terms included in Labov's paradigm (1972, 314, quoted in Beal 2010, 92). The description of upper-class English implies the very existence of such linguistic code; another objective is, in fact, that of demonstrating that the upper-class speech in the UK is

---

3 The main source followed in writing section III through an appropriate conceptual and terminological approach was Alan Brymance's manual *Social Research Methods* (2012), particularly the part dedicated to the nature and the techniques of qualitative research. The reading of the methodology-related chapter in *Audiovisual Translation: Theories, Methods and Issues* (2014) by Luis Pérez González was also very useful, because, even though this study is not specifically on AVT, the research methods described in his book can, in my opinion, also be applied to audiovisual texts in general.

a full diastratic variety and not just an 'upper' and more formal register. Moreover, anecdotal evidence from the frequent presence of aristocratic characters in films and TV series raised research questions on the relationship between the natural face-to-face language of the British nobility and its representation in audiovisual dialogue: are there any linguistic features that can contribute to create the upper-class social background of a character? Which are the features, among those that are commonly used, which make this type of speech sound either stereotypical or realistic?

All of these objectives will hopefully be achieved through a qualitative methodological approach. The above-mentioned research questions were stimulated by a personal interest in the field of sociolinguistics and are closely connected to the previous literature on the topic, being the main aim of this research that of modernising and systematising insightful but sparse or episodic data. The study of this literature was fundamental for the second step in this research, which was the selection of the texts to be analysed in order to both validate the evidence from previous works and add original data. Following the principles of Conversation Analysis, which is a traditional qualitative approach that has language as an object of study more than a medium (Sidnell 2009 and 2016), and whose techniques are partially adopted in this study, extreme care was dedicated to the process of transcription of the selected texts. Such texts are, in particular, audiovisual excerpts taken from documentaries, interviews and TV series episodes, and their attentive transcription served to guarantee a detailed analysis and an accurate collection of data, which were analysed through a sociophonetic approach (Thomas 2013). The last phase consisted in the interpretation and discussion of the collected data through an inductive method aimed at reaching a formal coding, namely the categorisation and organisation of data. The computer-assisted tool for the analysis of speech, WASP (Waveform, Annotations, Spectogram & Pitch), was also adopted in this phase to expand and to an extent validate personal interpretation.[4]

The research method adopted for this research can be considered, in other words, as an empirical archival method, whose three major steps

---

4   WASP is a free programme for the recording and analysis of speech. It can be used to display spectrograms, pitch marks, waveforms and frequency tracks. Its copyrights are owned by Mark Huckvale, University College London.

were the location, the inspection and the interpretation of the documentary sources.

IV. Description of the chapters

This volume is composed by two main parts: a theoretical one (Chapters 1 and 2) in which a complete framework on the topic of upper-class English will be provided, and an analytical one (Chapters 3, 4 and 5), whose outcomes will hopefully exemplify and add original insights to the academic research on the topic.

Apart from delineating issues related to the main purposes and methodological approaches of this research, this introduction also provided some basic knowledge on language variation and anticipated some information about the upper-class sociolect. The first chapter will provide a complete linguistic overview on this language variety, thus proving that upper-class English is not a mere 'posh' accent or old-fashioned register that speakers only adopt consciously to signal their status, but a real native social variety typical of a specific social group in Britain, bearing in mind that it is fundamentally very close to both Standard British English and Received Pronunciation.[5] In order to do so, all the aspects of linguistics will be taken into consideration, from phonology and prosody to morpho-syntax and lexis.

Chapter 2 will deal with upper-class English through a diachronic perspective by exploring its evolution throughout the last few centuries. After a brief overview on the rise of the prestigious form in Britain and on the features that were considered as symbols of an upper-class speech in the nineteenth century and the early twentieth century, the chapter will focus

---

5   The two definitions are often used interchangeably by non-specialists, but it is important to underline that they are not synonyms and they refer to two different concepts. In fact, while Standard British English (SBE) refers to the grammatical structures and vocabulary that we are usually taught in schools, Received Pronunciation (RP) is the accent that is traditionally regarded as standard. In other words, this difference mirrors the more general distinction between dialect and accent. Following Trudgill, we may dare to argue that while it is very likely to notice that any RP speaker also speaks SBE, most people who speak SBE have a regional pronunciation (1999, 3).

on the present-day situation of upper-class English, focusing on its internal variation according to such social parameters as age and gender, but also regional influences. Finally, a perspective on the possible future evolutions of this sociolect will be provided as a conclusive section of the theoretical part.

In the second part of the book, instances of upper-class speech will be analysed. First of all, Chapter 3 will be devoted to the English language as spoken by the members of the high society in real life. Transcriptions of audiovisual recordings of natural conversation featuring the members of the Royal Family will be analysed to verify if the scholars' taxonomies that are quoted in the first two chapters can be actually applied to real face-to-face dialogue. The Royal Family was chosen because it is the emblem of the British high society; also, it is a rather heterogeneous speech community in terms of age and gender, therefore it provides a fruitful discussion on the social variation of upper-class speech. A final section of this chapter will be devoted to the brief analysis of the speech of other British upper-class families, like the Mitfords, – the family of the same Nancy Mitford who approved the theorisation on what is 'U' or 'non-U' – to expand the discussion to members of the upper class who are not part of the royal speech community.

Chapter 4, on the other hand, will deal with the representation of upper-class English in samples of fictional audiovisual dialogue. A general overview of the topic will show that some linguistic features are recurrently used to portray the language of upper-class characters, showing a conscious awareness on the part of film creators of the existence of an aristocratic code; this code, as it will be explored, is often adopted in fictional dialogue to enrich the text with various kind of functions. The Netflix TV series *The Crown* (2016–present) will serve as a case study and it was chosen because it is one of the few products whose main characters are all almost exclusively members of the upper class; therefore, their language was not constructed to portray a stereotypical contrast with the members of the lower classes, but to create a realistic representation of British aristocracy. Both the analyses of the fictional dialogue selected from *The Crown* and that of natural dialogue taken from interviews to the members of the Royal Family will be conducted by adopting techniques related to the field of sociophonetics and conversation analysis.

Finally, Chapter 5 will be directly devoted to the comparison between natural and represented spoken language, through the linguistic analysis of some famous speeches delivered by Queen Elizabeth II and other aristocratic figures and their rendition in *The Crown*. The purpose of the chapter is descriptive and it will show which features were retained, omitted or modified in the difficult process of construction of the character identity through language. Moreover, it will be interesting to notice how speakers can consciously emphasise (or not) some features in public speeches in comparison with the act of conversation. In any case, since the representation of the Queen's speeches in the series was more or less literal, apart from minor cuts, the aspects that will be discussed in this chapter will be mostly phonological and prosodic. In some cases, data will be summed up in tables and diagrams generated through the WASP online tool, so as to show graphically what could otherwise only be noticed acoustically.

A conclusive discussion will follow, and the final considerations on the results of the research will hopefully shed a new light on the concept of upper-class English and open to new challenges "to more adequately embed the accents of elites into our understanding of the social stratification of language variation and change." (Britain 2017, 295).

Chapter 1 Classification and linguistic features of upper-class English

1.1. Upper-class speech and RP

Upper-class English has often been associated to Received Pronunciation (RP), but, while the general concept of RP has attracted the attention of numerous scholars in linguistics,[6] the language of the upper classes as such has been only scarcely investigated. RP has long been considered as the standard English accent, a prestige form to be taken as a model and accepted as a norm, even though its privileged status is not due to any intrinsic qualities, but it has been acquired for historical reasons (Wells 1998, 34–35). Before providing a further description of the accent, a brief discussion on the term RP will help outline a clearer definition of the concept of RP.

According to Wells, the name Received Pronunciation is "less than happy, relying as it does on an outmoded meaning of *received* ('generally accepted')" (1998, 117) and even phonetician Daniel Jones, who was the first one to codify its description, was not happy with the label (1960, 12); however, consciously or not, he established the term, whose first use was traditionally linked to Alexander Ellis but has more recently been ascribed to the eighteenth-century lexicographer John Walker (Mugglestone 2007, 258; Sturiale 2002, 91; Cruttenden 2014, 75). Jones described and codified RP mainly because he thought it was useful, if not even necessary, for intelligibility and language teaching purposes (Sturiale 2002, 94), but he also declared that the term did not imply that other accents were not equally 'good;' yet, he wrote his works at the beginning of the twentieth century, a period in which national broadcasting was developing and thus demanding for the spreading of a standard pronunciation (Cruttenden 2014, 77). The label Received Pronunciation began to be not only questioned but even rejected by the major linguists and dialectologists in the 1990s and the

---

6 For a complete description and discussion on RP, see, among others, Gimson 1984, Ramsaran 1990, Milroy 2001, Sturiale 2002, Roach 2004, Upton 2004, Santipolo 2006, Kerswill 2007, Trudgill 2008, Cruttenden 2014, Hinton 2015, Mugglestone 2017, Fabricius 2018, Beal 2020.

2000s, like Trudgill, Honey, the Milroys and Leith, as listed by Sturiale (2002, 95–96), because it implied the controversial concept of a standard accent. Peter Trudgill, in particular, proposed a different point of view, arguing that RP should not be considered as the standard English accent but rather as a standardised one (ibid.).

Although there has been a debate on the name of the accent and on its status as a model of spoken language in Britain, the phoneticians who first described it agreed on one aspect of the definition of RP, namely the fact that it is a prestigious accent: Ellis defined it as "the educated pronunciation of the metropolis" (1869, 23, quoted in Upton 2004, 217) and Jones as the speech of "the families of Southern English persons whose men-folk have been educated at the great public boarding schools" (1917, viii, quoted in Cruttenden 2014, 76). All the major linguists of twentieth century have later confirmed that RP is undoubtedly the accent of people in power, and those who have been educated in Public Schools (among others, Crystal 1995, 365; Wells 1998, 117; Trudgill 2000, 7). Therefore, RP has often been considered the pronunciation of the social élite, who generally "do not betray their geographical origins at all when they speak," while "people of a more middle-class background will tend to have more of a regional accent" (Trudgill 1994, 7).

However, all the linguists listed above never said explicitly that RP is the accent of the British upper classes – apart from Wells (1992), see next section. They only mentioned some of the characteristics of the RP speaker, such as a certain level of educatedness and the type of schools where they acquired it. Public schools are, in fact, often mentioned in association with RP, but while it is true that in the past only the sons of the noble families attended them, we cannot say the same about the contemporary age. More and more people in Britain have been able to guarantee an advanced and exclusive education to their children in the last several decades, despite not having a noble title, and this has been possible thanks to their access in the world of the professional jobs; but, as it was discussed in the introduction, occupation is not the only aspect that defines social stratifications. A high level of economic capital is not enough to define a person as part of the upper class, but they are characterised by same high levels of social and cultural capitals too (Savage et al. 2013, 225). Therefore, while it is true that RP is generally spoken in public schools, it should not be taken for granted that all the students that attend public schools nowadays have an 'upper' socio-cultural background.

The term 'upper-class' is rarely mentioned in sociolinguistic research, and the upper-class group is hardly ever included in the tests for sociolinguistic field studies, as it was also argued by Fabricius:

> Pioneering survey-based studies such as Labov (1963, 2006), Trudgill (1972), and Macaulay (1977) concentrated on data from speakers in the middle of the social hierarchy. Upper-class speakers were often not included in survey samples, or were the subject of particularised studies (Kroch 1995), and as a result were regarded as much less interesting for mainstream variationist work for a long time, seen as being far from the locus of sociolinguistic change, conservative followers rather than first-movers (2018, 38).

Despite not conducting quantitative studies on the speech of the upper-class people, some scholars in variationist sociolinguistics have referred to the issue of social class in identifying different varieties of RP. Wells, for example, argued that "no accent is a homogeneous invariant monolith – certainly not RP" (1992, 279) and proposed some subgroupings, which can be considered, says Agha, as "metadiscursive labels to name discursive varieties," which "personify speech by linking sound patterns to attributes of speakers" (2003, 234). According to Wells, upper-class people in England speak what can be named as Upper-crust RP, or simply U-RP, which is distinguished from the "central tendency," the so-called Mainstream RP (1992, 279). He provides some concrete reference to society to better highlight the difference between the two variants:

> The accent popularly associated with, say, a dowager duchess is not quite the same as mainstream RP. [...] The same applies to the speech of many upper-class army officers; to that of a Noel Coward sophisticate;[7] to that of a Terry Thomas cad;[8] to that of the popular image of an elderly Oxbridge don; and to that of a jolly-hockey-sticks schoolmistress at an expensive private girls' school. These all differ somewhat from one another as well as from the duchess. It is difficult in these matters to separate stereotype from reality, but it is reasonable to claim that these versions of RP are conspicuous in a way which makes it impossible to regard them as part of mainstream RP. Furthermore, they share an important

---

7   Noel Coward was an English playwright and actor, who had a public image of elegance and sophistication.

8   Terry Thomas was an English actor who often portrayed infamous upper-class characters.

social characteristic: they are, in the narrow sense, upper-class. They are not middle-class (ibid., 280).

It can be thus inferred that, while U-RP is the accent of the upper class, mainstream RP is the accent of the upper-middle class and it is the one that everybody in Britain is familiar with and that people are taught either as L1 or L2; U-RP, on the contrary, has some specific phonetic features which will be explored in section 1.3.1. However, both the variants share the fact that they are native accents, because, despite being often the reference accent in school education, those who did not acquire RP as children but only later in their life speak what Wells defines as Adoptive RP. This label refers to the speech of those who experienced a change in their social circumstances and who feel some kind of need to conform to a 'regionless' accent. Adoptive RP, Wells explains, can perfectly merge imperceptibly into Mainstream RP, but speakers of this variant may show a lack of control in informal situations and a tendency to avoid phenomena that Mainstream-RP speakers frequently use in those contexts, e.g., elision, assimilation, smoothing (ibid. 284). Adoptive RP is to be distinguished from Near-RP,[9] which is an umbrella term for any accents which "while not falling within the definition of RP, nevertheless includes very little in the way of regionalisms which would enable the provenance of the speaker to be localized within England" (ibid. 297) and can be considered either a trace of 'provincialism' by an upper-class person, or of 'educatedness' by the rest of the population, making it a middle-class accent.

This study will deal specifically with U-RP, the accent that corresponds to the upper-class sociolect in Britain. The same accent has been named with different labels, and even Wells's classification was, in fact, a reinterpretation and expansion of the one proposed by Gimson (1970), who made a distinction between the neutral General RP and two variants that can be both considered in association with the upper classes, namely Conservative RP, mainly used by the older generations, and Advanced RP, "mainly used by young people of exclusive social groups – mostly of the upper classes,

---

9 Near-RP might be confused with Quasi-RP, another term proposed by Wells to indicate the result of "a speech training of a particularly unrealistic kind" (1992, 285).

but also, for prestige value, in certain professional circles" and it can "be judged 'affected' by other RP speakers, in the same way that all RP types are liable to be considered affected by those who use unmodified regional speech" (ibid., 88).

Upton (2004, 219) mentioned other two alternative proposals, Ramsaran's Traditional RP (1990) and Cruttenden's Refined RP (1994), but he did not deal extensively with the concept behind these labels. More recently, Cruttenden has changed his proposal into Conspicuous General British (CGB), building on the idea that the acronym GB, coined by Windsor Lewis in 1972, should be preferred to the old-fashioned RP (2014, 80–81). He described CGB as a 'posh' accent, to be associated with upper-class families and those professions which "have traditionally recruited from such families, e.g., officers in the navy [...]" (ibid.) and he emphasised the fact that the number of these speakers "has considerably declined in the last fifty years and is now mainly limited to older speaker" (ibid.).

In the course of this volume the accent of the British upper class will be referred to as U-RP, following Wells (1992, 280), for three main reasons. First of all, among all the works previously cited, Wells's was the only one to provide an extensive list of phonological features, thus carrying out a more systematic and concrete description of the accent. Secondly, the term U-RP makes explicit reference to the social class that generally adopts it, and, although the expression 'upper crust' might be considered colloquial, it creates a direct link between the linguistic and the social aspect, which is among the objectives of this research. Finally, it was chosen to adopt Wells's term also because it was later adopted by other linguists who dedicated part of their discussions to the upper-class accent, making it a well-established label in the scholarly literature (among others, Agha 2003; Britain 2017; Ranzato 2017 and 2018; Fabricius 2018; Richards 2018).

This study aims to emphasise the idea that, although it is fundamentally true that upper-class people in Britain speak Standard English with a Received Pronunciation, this statement needs a further specification; members of the high society, in fact, generally speak a specific variety of RP, which is frequently combined with a series of specific linguistic habits from the morpho-syntactic and lexical point of view. In other words, as Fabricius puts it, the British upper classes have their own vernacular, and this élite/establishment sociolect, while being closely related to the standard language, is to be distinguished from it (2018, 38–40).

> The tendency has been that upper-class groups' sociolect and the standard language were often assumed to be identical [...]. This ignores the fact that, first, upper-class and upper-middle-class speakers, of course, do acquire their own vernacular (meaning primarily language of socialisation), and that successive generations of such speakers exhibit vernacular variation and change over time (ibid.).

Fabricius herself had already tackled the issue of the distinction between the standard language and the élite sociolect by proposing the terms construct-RP (c-RP) and native-RP (n-RP). It is with this last label that the scholar identifies the linguistic patterns of the social group occupying the highest socio-economic niche in the stratified society. Moreover, she adds that this c-RP/n-RP separation is fundamental because "there is simply an acute empirical gap in understanding the sociolinguistic makeup of a class-stratified society if elite sociolect speakers are not represented" (ibid.). To further explain this separation, she also referred to Agha's concept of enregisterment (2003, 2007), which is defined as a collective perception and representation of a language variety that remains stable across time and places, thus becoming fixed, 'enregistered.' Linguistic features have no inherent social meaning, but they acquire it once they are enregistered (Agha 2003, 269, also quoted in Beal 2010, 94–95), and this is what has happened to U-RP, which has been recognised over time by all the Britons as a form of RP with some specific peculiarities, thanks to a "metadiscursive activity typifying accent forms and values" (Agha 2007, 196); for example, quoting Honey (1989), Agha refers to the misspellings of words in media which are transcribed as they are supposedly pronounced by U-RP speakers (ibid., 197).

The misspellings in Table 1 highlight one feature in particular of U-RP, namely the tendency to raise vowel sounds, which will be further explored in section 1.3.1. Whether these 'enregistered' forms are real indicators and markers of U-RP or stereotypical forms[10] (ibid.) will also be explored later on, but they were mentioned here to emphasise on the fact that upper-class

---

10 Indicators, markers and stereotypes are the three categories of the Labovian paradigm (Labov 1972), which is useful to classify linguistic variables according to their value in a specific speech community and to what extent speakers are aware of these evaluations. This theory was summed up by Beal (2010, 92), who explains: The categories can be seen as representing different stages in linguistic

Table 1 – Word spelling of U-RP (Honey1989, quoted in Agha 2007, 197)

Spelling used for U-RP words	Standard spelling
kebinet office	cabinet office
clawth	cloth
crawss	cross
lawft	loft
hape	hope
arm-air	army
fah	fire
pah of the British empah	power of the British empire
stains	stones

speech in Britain is highly recognisable and constitutes a well-defined variety of Received Pronunciation, characterised by a set of features that are generally automatically perceived as being distinctive of the social élite.

1.2. Upper-class style, social network and speech community

As it was mentioned in the introduction, there are not many sociolinguistic studies on upper-class English and the only one entirely devoted to it is, to my knowledge, Kroch's investigation (1996) on the language of upper-class people in Philadelphia. In his article, the scholar writes:

> The properties that distinguish upper class speech are not phonemic but prosodic and lexical. They constitute what Hymes (1974) calls a 'style' rather than a dialect. In particular, upper class speech is characterized by a drawling and laryngealized voice quality and, contrastingly, by frequent use of emphatic accent patterns and of intensifying modifiers. These features are iconic and have, perhaps for that reason, an intense interactional effect, at least on outsiders; and

> change: an incoming form becomes an indicator when it has been adopted by all members of a subgroup; it becomes a marker when it has spread throughout the speech community and been assigned a common value by that community such that style-shifting occur; finally, "under extreme stigmatization, a form may become the overt object of social comment, and may eventually disappear. It is thus a stereotype, which may become increasingly divorced from the forms which are actually used in speech" (Labov 1972:180) (ibid.).

this effect has led to the public recognition of the upper class speech style as distinctive (ibid., 39).

Saying that upper-class speech is to be considered as a style means that it
depends on the communicative situation rather than on the speaker, making
it a diaphasic variation and not a diastratic one. In fact, the difference
between a style and a dialect/sociolect is that the former is an intra-speaker
variation associated with the communicative setting (e.g., formal situations),
while the latter is an inter-speaker variation which is closely related to the
socio-demographic and biological characteristics of the speaker. In other
words, as Hallidayan linguistics puts it, a style is a mere aesthetic option
with no functional value in the communicative process. The term 'style' has
sometimes been used interchangeably with the term 'register,' but Labovian
sociolinguistics defines the latter as a lexical variety related to a particular
subject matter, often occupational (Coupland 2007, 9–18; Hernández-
Campoy 2016, 33–36). The fundamental differences between the concept
of style and that of sociolect are summed up in Table 2.

Table 2 – Difference between style and sociolect (summed up from Hernández-
Campoy 2016, building on Labov 1972, Halliday 1978 and Trudgill 2006)

style	sociolect
o diaphasic axis	o diastratic axis
o intra-speaker variation	o inter-speaker variation
o variation according to the use (the communicative setting)	o variation according to the user (social characteristics)
o aesthetic value	o functional value

Although one of the aims of this research is to emphasise that upper-
class English in Britain can and should be considered as a sociolect, defined
by all of the points listed in the corresponding column in Table 2, there is
no implicit intention to deny the fact that upper-class speech can also be
adopted as a speech style. Sociolects and styles are often closely connected
and, according to Romaine (2000, 75), such correlation is one of the
most meaningful findings of quantitative sociolinguistics inasmuch as the
frequency of specific linguistic features can be, at times, a marker of both

social class and situation (ibid.). Linguistic varieties are usually assigned a certain social function, and each speaker possesses a verbal repertoire of different variants with different social meanings, making him/her multidialectal and able to switch from one variety to another according to different communicative contexts (Hernández-Campoy 2016, 38, quoting Clyne 2004 and Trudgill 2006); yet, having recourse to linguistic expedients that are specific of a language variety to manipulate one's own style does not exclude that there are other speakers who use that same variety with no intention of accommodating their speech to a specific social situation. For instance, standardness is generally associated with formality (Trudgill 1994, 11 and 2000, 94), but there are people – for example speakers of English as L2 – who adopt Standard English as their natural every-day language, and this also admits variation in style. The same applies to upper-class English, which is a social-class dialect, but some of its features can either be adopted by 'non-U' native speakers or emphasised by 'U' speakers to achieve the so-called 'formal style,' which is the speaking modality in which, according to Labov (2006, 59), the speaker takes conscious control over his/her speech (in contraposition with the 'casual style,' ibid.). Both cases are events of 'style shifting,' a linguistic phenomenon that occurs when the speaker has a social reaction to a situation and has a relatively high level of attention on his/her speech (Hernández-Campoy and Cutillas-Espinosa, 2012, 1–18). According to Bell (1984, 1997), who developed the Audience Design framework, style shifting can be defined more specifically as the speakers' response to a change in their audience. Such framework, as suggested by Mason (1997), is also relevant in screen dialogue.

Evidence of style shifting can happen for several reasons, but in the case of a shifting towards an upper-class/'posh'/elevated style two main motives can be identified: one is the cultural prestige of the élite social group and, consequently, of its way of speaking, and the other is the group identification through language. Language, in fact, is not only a means of communicating, and language acts are often to be considered as acts of identity too; as Chambers (2003) puts it "the underlying cause of sociolinguistic differences, largely beneath consciousness, is the human instinct to establish and maintain social identity" (ibid., 274). In other words, speakers often modulate their language so that they feel part of a network.

A 'social network' is an aggregate of relationships and personal ties among people whose structure can also be maintained through language if the network is constituted by strong, 'dense' ties (Milroy and Llamas 2013, 410).

> A network can be described as dense when, in a given group of persons, virtually everybody knows everybody. Ties of this kind typically exist in small territorial communities such as villages and in well-defined urban communities [...]. But they may also exist at higher levels of society, e.g. in professional sub-groups and in upper-class society, where contacts may be maintained over long distances owing to important common interests (Milroy and Milroy 1999, 49).[11]

Strong ties can act as norm-enforcement mechanisms and they are taken into consideration in social science research in the process of identification of patterns for vernacular maintenance (Milroy and Milroy 1997, 59), as it also resulted from pioneering studies in the field such as Milroy and Milroy's sociolinguistic investigation in Belfast inner-city (1987) and Labov's study in Martha's Vineyard (1960).[12] Both cases show how "it is evident that close-knit solidarity ties are characteristic of lower and higher social groups, and that, in the middle sectors of society, social network density and multiplexity tend to be weak" (Milroy and Milroy 1997, 61).

Social-network analysis deals with the variability in individual linguistic behaviour, but quantitative sociolinguistics can also focus on larger scale investigation of communities. Upper-class people can be considered an example of speech community in a Labovian sense (1972), namely as a

---

11 The sociolinguistic concept of dense social network partly overlaps with that of community of practice, but they differ in terms of the kind of membership, which is generally a matter of circumstance in the first case and more conscious in the second (Meyerhof-Strycharz 2013, 432).

12 Martha's Vineyard's case is particularly interesting, because Labov's study (1960) showed that people living on the island, who are generally quite wealthy, tend to exaggerate their old-fashioned raised pronunciation of some vowel sounds, especially diphthongs, as an identity marker (Hernández-Campoy 2016, 54). This feature is, as it will be explored in the next section, one of the most defining features of U-RP in UK.

group of people sharing a set of norms that are often observed in evaluative behaviour. According to this kind of attitude towards language, some of the individuals in the upper-class community may decide to make abundant use of certain linguistic features in order to reaffirm their position inside the social network they believe they belong to. Likewise, people who are not part of the same community and/or network, but aspire to enter it, might decide to acquire a certain kind of speech style. In this case, we may talk of what Agha (2007) defines as 'strategic stylization,' which occurs when a style has become enregistered and is part of a metapragmatic model (ibid, 185–188).

The aim of this section was that of clarifying in sociolinguistic terms that we can consider upper-class English as a sociolect, yet its main linguistic features can also be adopted to affect an upper-class speech style in certain social contexts, and also, for instance, to portray 'posh' characters in fictional audiovisual productions. What will follow in the rest of the chapter is a complete list of all these features.

1.3. Linguistic features

Upper-class English may be succinctly defined as Standard British English spoken with an upper-crust RP, considering that, as it was mentioned in the previous sections, the most defining aspects of this sociolect are phonological and prosodic. There are, however, linguistic habits from the lexical and morphosyntactic point of few that are generally recognised as specific of the British élite and that will be listed after a complete outline of the most salient features of U-RP.

1.3.1. U-RP: phonological and prosodic features

The label upper-crust RP, as previously mentioned, was introduced by John C. Wells (1992, 280–283), who is also, at present, the only linguist who has provided a list of the most salient phonological characteristics that are generally found in the speech of upper-class people in Britain. Building on his list, but also on his insights on the pronunciation of the single lexical sets (1998, 127–167 and 212–241), this section aims at expanding it by examining innovations, evolutions and new evidence.

• *Vowels:*

Vowel sounds in U-RP are generally 'raised'[13] compared to Mainstream RP, and the vowel in TRAP words[14] is perhaps one of the most recognisable features. In this lexical set, the near-open front vowel /æ/ is often diphthonged as [ɛæ], or even [eæ], e.g. "that man" ['ðɛæt 'mɛæn]. The analysis of the case studies will point out that it is also often pronounced as [ɛ]. Wells also adds that this feature, once widely used, is now outmoded and less used by the younger generations in favour of the open central vowel [a]. Some scholars have recently noticed that the realisation of the TRAP vowel in U-RP has become partially closer to the mainstream-RP pronunciation, as resulted from the acoustic analysis of some speeches by the Queen (Harrington et al. 2000; Fabricius 2007; Richards 2018 – see Chapter 3 for a more extended discussion on the topic).

The open HAPPY vowel is another sound which is generally widely recognised as being specific of U-RP, as many representations of U-RP speakers in film and TV productions show (see Chapter 4 for a wider discussion on this). The final vowel in words like 'happy' had always been described as being [ɪ] before Gimson (1962) first noticed that that phoneme was being progressively replaced by [iː] (Wells 1998, 257–258). Such phenomenon, known as Happy Tensing, has led to the introduction of /iː/ as a new standard and has also affected U-RP, which has now acquired [ɪ] as an alternative to the old-fashioned [ɛ], still occasionally found especially in utterance-final position. Wells comments that the strikingly open HAPPY vowel is always found, for instance, in the enclitic 'me' (1992, 281). As it was suggested by Harrington (2006), the HAPPY vowel in U-RP is still closer to that in KIT words rather than FLEECE words because the second

---

13 Saying that vowels are 'raised' in U-RP means that the speakers of this accent generally use sounds that are placed in a higher position on the vowel chart. For example, where a Mainstream-RP speaker uses an open vowel, a U-RP speaker uses an open-mid vowel.

14 Several words in small capitals are used throughout the whole volume, especially in this section. These words are conventionally called 'standard lexical sets' and are used as keywords in phonological studies to refer to group of words with the same sound; thus, for instance, words like 'tap,' 'cat,' 'back,' etc. are included in the TRAP lexical set (Wells 1998, xviii–xix).

case is considered to be a marker of Estuary English, a Southern English variety that has been influenced by Cockney, so it might be resisted because socially marked (ibid., 454).

It is old-fashioned, says Wells (1992, 282), but also still used by the younger generation when they want to emphasise their belonging to the élite, the realisation of [ɔ:] instead of /ɒ/ in the CLOTH lexical set; thus, for example, 'off' [ɔ:f]. Curiously, U-RP shares with General American[15] the use of the same vowel as THOUGHT in the CLOTH set (Wells 1998, 160), although it is at times "perceived as laughable" (ibid. 236). Finally, another monophthong which is very open in U-RP, compared to the mainstream variety, is NURSE [nɐ:s] rather than /n3:s/ (ibid.).

Diphthongal sounds are also subject to some phenomena in U-RP. In particular, the centring diphthongs in NEAR, SQUARE and CURE, whose standard pronunciations are /ɪə, ɜə, ʊə/, have a very open second element when in free position, thus [nɪɑ, skwɜɑ, kjʊɑ] (Wells 1992, 281). Instead, in other cases like PRICE and MOUTH, the phenomenon of 'smoothing' may occur in U-RP, namely the monophthonging process of /aɪ, aʊ/ into [a:], which, as mentioned – although not widely explored – by Wells, the upper-class speech shares with Cockney (1998, 239). Ross (1959) also confirms that "some U-speakers pronounce *tyre* and *tar* identically (and so for many other words, such as *fire* – even going to the length of making *lion* rhyme with *barn*)" (ibid., 17).

The same vocalic features listed in this section are also found is Wales's (1994, 4–5) description of the language variety that she calls 'Royalese.'

• *Consonants*:

As far as consonants are concerned, the most recognisable feature of U-RP is the use of tapped /ɾ/ in intervocalic position, as in 'very sorry' [vɜɾɪ sɒɾɪ], whereas in Mainstream RP a retroflex /ɹ/ is found. Nowadays, it is very rare in modern speech and it is used perhaps only by the older generation (Fabricius 2018, 51), but it is one the main features that is used in telecinematic representations of the aristocracy. It is probably for this

---

15 General American (GenAm) is the expression that is generally used to indicate the English language as spoken by people in the United States who do not have a recognisable local accent.

reason and due to British people who became prominent in the US, like playwright and actor Noël Coward, Wells argues, that most Americans have the impression that [ɾ] is the usual British realisation of /r/ (1992, 282). Speaking about old-fashioned affectations of U-RP and stereotypical representations, Wells (ibid.) mentions that intervocalic /r/ can also be rarely rendered with the labiodental approximant [ʋ][16] or the labiovelar approximant [w]. At times, but restricted to a small group of common words like 'very' and 'terribly,' a total elision of /r/ can be noticed, thus [vɜ.ɪ, tɜ.ɪblɪ] (ibid.).

The realisation of /r/ as a vibrant sound rather than an approximant one is considered, in associations with other features, a trace of some regional varieties of British English, such as some Northern and South-Western accents, and, interestingly, this is not the only consonantal feature that U-RP shares with lower-status accents. It is not rare, in fact, to hear U-RP speakers pronounce the '-ing' variable as [ɪn], with an alveolar rather than a velar nasal /ɪŋ/ (Wells 1992, 283). As in some of the cases that were previously mentioned, the [ɪn] variant is also an old-fashioned use, showing a conservative attitude of the upper-class members towards language innovations; [ɪn] was, in fact, fashionable in the eighteenth century and was then replaced by the /ɪŋ/ innovation, whereas it "remains in English folk-memory as the U-RP stereotype of *huntin', shootin', and fishin'*" (Wells 1998, 262).

Other phonological phenomena that are sometimes associated with regional or low-status dialects, such as T-glottalisation and H-dropping, are by all means avoided by the élite; the sounds /t/ (but also of the other voiceless plosives, /p, k/) and /h/ are always clearly pronounced, and, at times, even emphasised. Such emphasis sometimes causes other phenomena, like the nasal release that can be heard when /p, t, k/ are followed by a nasal (e.g., 'cotton') or when the same consonants are initials of a stressed syllable and have a little aspiration, making the sound even more 'plosive.' (ibid., 282). As previously mentioned, it is true that /t/ is neither glottalled nor glottalised, but, as Wells puts it, when it is in preconsonantal position

---

16 As an Italian mother-tongue speaker, I dare suggest that [ʋ] is the sound that is also generally used to affect a stereotypical posh accent in Italian in some words containing the intervocalic /r/, e.g., *tesoro* [tezɔʋo].

it "is articulated in a way which accommodates to, or overlaps with, the following segment" (ibid.). Moreover, although it is not listed in Wells's taxonomy, it can be added the /t/ is often subject to affrication when in utterance-final position, as in 'do it' [dʊ ɪtʃ].[17]

As regards the glottal fricative /h/, its use in initial stressed position is defined by Wells as "the single most powerful pronunciation shibboleth in England" (1998, 254) and by Mugglestone as a "symbol of social divide" (2007, 95). In particular, its clear realisation is inevitably associated with the "educated" and "polite," while its omission is generally felt as a "vulgar," "ignorant" and a lower-class feature (ibid.). The social implications of H-dropping became particularly strong in the course of the nineteenth century (ibid., 95–134), and even those h-words that had an original /h/-less pronunciation in RP are now pronounced with a restored /h/, although there is one word which still has an /h/-less form in U-RP: 'hotel' [əʊtel] (Wells 1998, 255); this is also confirmed by Ross (1959), who adds it is also to be considered 'U' to drop /h/ in 'humour' (ibid., 17). The same lack of /h/ applies to the personal pronouns 'he,' 'his,' 'him,' 'her,' when in post-pausal position (e.g., 'tell him' [telɪm]), but Wells explains that these are not to be considered cases of H-dropping because the h-syllables are not stressed; on the contrary, the insertion of /h/ in cases similar to the example provided can be found in utterances by "some middle-class speakers, perhaps in a genteel anxiety not to do something so vulgar as dropping an /h/" (ibid.).

Finally, Cruttenden (2014) argues that another innovation that is recently taking place in modern English, the Yod Dropping ('tune' pronounced as [tuːn] instead of /tjuːn/) never occurs in U-RP, or, as he calls it, Conspicuous General British (ibid., 81).

---

17 At the time of writing, no reference to this phenomenon has been found in previous scholars' studies on the accent of the upper classes. My contention is based on anecdotal evidence on the representation of upper-class people in audiovisual products, although I believe this is not a stereotyped feature but rather an indicator of upper-class speech in real life that some filmmakers have consciously noticed and reproduced; such evidence will be shown and further explored in the analysis of the case studies in Chapters 3 and 4; see also Valleriani 2021 (196-199).

• *Prosody and voice quality:*

Suprasegmental phonology is perhaps one of the most defining aspects of upper-class English; intonation, stressing and voice quality all contribute in making the speech of the British élite highly recognisable.

The first characteristic that Wells (1992) mentions as being frequent in U-RP is the "prolonging of the steady-state of a consonant" (ibid., 283), which, he adds, is usually noticeable when a voiceless consonant follows an accented vowel, as in 'frightfully' ['fraɪtːflɪ] and 'awfully' ['ɔːflɪ]. Such phenomenon generally conveys an emphatic effect to the speech.

Another peculiar rhythmic pattern due to a variation in sound lengthening is found in words with a penultimate stress. In words like 'water,' 'wider' or 'reducing,' the stressed vowels are sometimes shorter than the final unstressed one in U-RP, and, building on this notion, Wells (ibid.) proposes that the word 'parking-meter' might be taken as a shibboleth to find out if a speaker is member of the upper class or not. As he puts it,

> In U-RP the [ɪŋ] of parking is considerably longer than the [ɑː], and the [ə] of meter longer than the [iː] – in spite of what the conventional use of length-marks suggests. When I put a U-RP accent for purposes of acting, demonstration, or caricature, I find that this is one of the obvious changes I make in my ordinary speech (ibid.).

Not only the duration of the stress, but also the variation of its position in some words can serve to distinguish a 'U' from a 'non-U' speaker, as pointed out by Ross (1959); for instance, he mentions that 'temporarily' and 'interesting' are pronounced with an accented first vowel by upper-class speakers, thus ['tɜmprərəlɪ, 'ɪntrəstɪn], causing a reduction of the number of the syllables compared to the more-widely-spread forms 'temporàrily' and 'interèsting' (ibid., 16, but see also Wales 1994, 4).

Speaking of voice quality, on the other hand, Wells (1992) states that another feature that he admits he affects when imitating a U-RP voice is the lowering of the larynx and widening of the oro-pharynx, which he calls 'plumminess'[18] (ibid., 283). Cruttenden (2014) further argues that both the tongue and the jaw acquire a more open position than in the Mainstream-RP speakers, which is why vowel sounds are generally rather open (ibid., 81, also quoted in Ranzato 2017, 31).

---

18 As explained in Ranzato (2017), the term means that U-RP speakers sound as if they had 'a plum in their mouth' (ibid., 31).

Other expressions that are usually heard in reference to the effect conveyed by upper-class voices are 'crisp and clipped' and 'cut glass.' The former is an expression which comes from the use of tapped [ɾ] (Wells 1992, 282) and which is perceived as being "languid and effete" (Ranzato 2018, 207), while the latter is generally used to indicate an accent with a clear articulation of each single word.

*

Before dealing with the lexical and morpho-syntactic characteristics of upper-class English, a summative table containing the main acoustic features of this accent is provided, building especially on Wells's insights on the topic (1992 and 1998) but also partially on Ross (1959), Wales (1994), Harrington et al. (2000), Fabricius (2007), Mugglestone (2007), Cruttenden (2014), Ranzato (2017 and 2018), Richards (2018), and personal anecdotal evidence:[19]

Table 3 – Phonological features of U-RP

Features of upper-crust RP	Counterpart in mainstream RP
diphthongisation of TRAP vowel: [tɹɛæp]	/tɹæp/
open HAPPY vowel: [hæpɪ]	/hæpiː/
raised CLOTH vowel: [klɔːθ]	/klɒθ/
open diphthongs in NEAR, SQUARE, CURE: [nɪɑ, skwɜɑ, kjʊɑ]	/nɪə, skwɜə, kjʊə/
smoothing in PRICE: [pɹaːs]	/pɹaɪs/
tapped 'R' in intervocalic position: 'sorry' [sɒɾi]	/sɒɹi/
[ɪn] variant: 'hunting' [hʌntɪn]	/hʌntɪŋ/
affrication of /t/ in utterance-final position: [ɪtʃ]	/ɪt/
emphatic intonation through the prolonging of voiceless consonants after an accented vowel: 'frightfully' [fraɪtːflɪ]	/fraɪtfəlɪ/
unstressed vowels longer than stressed vowels; 'parking-meter' [pɑkɪːn mitə:]	/ pɑːkɪn miːtə/
lowering of the larynx and widening of the oropharynx ('plumminess')	larynx in mid position

---

19 Some of the phenomena listed in Table 3 can be heard at https://pronunciation-studio.com/upper-received-pronunciation/ (last accessed 12/09/2020).

1.3.2. Morpho-syntactic features

From the viewpoint of the morphological and syntactical aspects of the language, there is not much to point out about the upper-class sociolect. Members of the high society, in fact, generally use a perfect Standard English both in spoken and written language, since it is also thanks to the prestige of the dialect of the upper classes that a standard was born in Britain (see Chapter 2 for a historical outline).

It was shown in the previous section, in fact, that the main aspect that defines the language of the upper-class people is their accent, called by Wells (1992) as upper-crust RP. However, Wells (ibid.) also mentions one grammatical feature that is often found in utterances by aristocratic speakers, namely the use of the weak pronoun 'me' instead of the possessive 'my.' Its phonological realisation is frequently [mɪ], but it can also be [mə]. Wells says that, despite being generally considered as a low-status characteristic, it is possible to hear that "at Eton one addresses one's tutor as [mə'tjuːtə]" (ibid., 283).

Fox (2004), while 'revisiting' the 'U/non-U' dichotomy (see next session), mentions that another interesting peculiarity of upper-class English is the tendency to avoid personal pronouns in general, when possible, and especially 'I,' arguing that at the highest level of society "one prefers to refer to oneself as 'one'" (ibid., 204). The same aspect was also studied by Wales (1994), who defined it as the 'royal one;' according to the scholar, the use of 'one' as a variant of both 'I' and the impersonal 'you' is noted in the utterances of various members of the Royal Family and some of their close friends and members of their personnel (ibid., 9), and she argues that it can be considered as a replacement of the obsolete 'royal we,' popularly associated with Queen Victoria, who often referred to herself with 'we' instead of 'I' (ibid., 8). The egocentric use of 'one' "has in the latter part of the twentieth century acquired connotations of upper classness, and, to non-users, connotations of pretentiousness and affectation" (ibid., 9), so much so that, as pointed out by Goodman (1997), in the 1990s it was not rare to read it on tabloid headlines to mimic the language of the Royal Family. This feature is also frequently adopted in the fictional representations of the Queen's language, both in literature and cinema, as Di Martino (2012) observed in her analysis of *The Uncommon Reader* (2007) by Alan Bennett (ibid., 63–73), and she also mentioned that an occasional use of 'one' instead of 'I' can be heard in Stephen Frears's film *The Queen* (2006), whose script was written by Peter Morgan (ibid., 69).

Not much else is said about grammar peculiarities of upper-class English in previous studies related to the topic, but a few other points can be added here as findings coming from personal analysis of recordings featuring this sociolect (see Chapters 3 and 4). In particular, it can be safely argued that the conservative attitude towards language by the members of the upper classes is traced in the use of some old-fashioned structures, such as the modal 'shall' to indicate the future form for the first persons. Also, 'may' seems to be generally preferred to 'can' not only in formal situations, but also in informal conversation, and 'should' is sometimes heard as a substitute of 'must.'

Finally, an abundant use of emphatic qualifying adverbs can be noted in utterances by upper-class people, such as 'extremely,' 'frightfully,' 'awfully,' 'terribly,' 'utterly,' 'ghastly' (Wales 1994, 7).

1.3.3. Lexical features[20]

Apart from the concept itself of defining linguistic attitudes as 'U' or 'non-U,' the part of Ross's article (1959) that has caused most of the controversy (see the introduction) is probably the section dedicated to vocabulary (ibid., 17–19). Part of the debate was that some of Ross's indications for 'U' language were starting to be felt as old-fashioned even at the time of his writing. The reasons why certain words ceased to be used by upper-class people, too, in favour of their 'non-U' counterparts, are either related to social changes – words like 'looking-class' started to be perceived as pretentious – or technological changes – the old 'U' word 'wireless' is no longer used to call the radio for obvious reasons (Taggart 2010, 11–12). Moreover, as mentioned in the introduction, Ross's indications are not grounded in a scientific method, but they are rather the result of his personal observation and opinion. Part of his indications, in particular, are taken from the novel *The Pursuit of Love* (1945) by Nancy Mitford, and the following passage seems to have especially inspired him:

> Uncle Matthew: 'Education! I was always led to suppose that no educated person ever spoke of notepaper, and yet I hear poor Fanny asking Sadie for notepaper. What is this education? Fanny talks about mirrors and mantelpieces, hand-bags

---

20 Due to the lack of a real scholarly literature on the topic, section 1.3.3 builds mainly on online articles and mainstream jargon-free works.

and perfume, she takes sugar in her coffee, has a tassel on her umbrella, and I have no doubts that, 'if she is ever fortunate enough to catch a husband, she will call his father and mother Father and Mother. Will the wonderful education she is getting make up to the unhappy brute for all these endless pinpricks? Fancy hearing one's wife talk about notepaper – the irritation!'

   Aunt Emily: 'A lot of men would find it more irritating to have a wife who had never heard of George III. (All the same, Fanny darling, it is called writing-paper, you know – don't let's hear any more about the note, please.) That is where you and I come in, you see, Matthew, home influence is admitted to be a most important part of education.' (1949, 31).

There are, however, a few words mentioned by Alan Ross that are still perceived as lexical shibboleths for upper-class language, as pointed out by Fox (2004), Taggart (2010) and Bell (2019). It is also interesting to cite an anonymous article on the website *The Lady*,[21] whose title is "Pardon? That's practically a swear word," which refers to the stigma of the word 'pardon' in the upper strata of society. Fox argues that " 'pardon' is the most notorious pet hate of the upper and upper-middle class" and that members of the lower classes might use it "in a misguided attempt to sound 'posh' " (2004, 211–212). This happens, says Ross, "(1) if the hearer does not hear the speaker properly; (2) as an apology [...]; (3) after hiccupping or belching. The normal U-correspondences are very curt, viz. (1) *What?* (2) *Sorry!* (3) [Silence][22] [...]" (1959, 18).

   Another word that, to an upper-class ear, marks the speaker as 'non-U' is 'toilet.' This word, unlike 'pardon,' is rather neutral and used in everyday language, but upper-class people are very reluctant about its use and prefer the words 'lavatory' or 'loo' instead. All of the other alternatives (e.g., 'bathroom,' 'facilities,' etc.) are "suburban genteel euphemisms" used by lower classes with aspirations (Fox 2004, 212–213). As a consequence, upper-class people use 'lavatory-paper' rather than 'toilet-paper' (Ross 1959, 19; Taggart 2010, 13).

   Fox (2004) includes 'pardon' and 'toilet' in the list of the "Seven Deadly Sins," which are the "seven words that the English uppers and upper-middles

21 The article can be read at the following link: https://lady.co.uk/pardon-thats-practically-swear-word (last accessed 12/09/2020).
22 The above-mentioned article on *The Lady* quotes Nancy Mitford, who said "Silence is the only possible U-response to many embarrassing modern situations."

regard as infallible shibboleths" (ibid., 211–220). Among the others we find 'serviette,'[23] 'settee,' 'lounge,' which are working-class words for the more common 'napkin,' 'sofa' and 'sitting room.'[24] Finally, she also includes in the list the words 'dinner' and 'sweet,' which are not inappropriate in general, but only when used in certain contexts. 'Dinner' should not be used to refer to the midday meal, which is to be called 'lunch' (or 'luncheon' by the older upper-class generation); 'dinner,' in fact, is the name of the evening meal (also 'supper' if the meal is a light one), which is at times called 'tea' by the working-class. In the upper-class contexts, 'tea' is the mid-afternoon refreshment and, since it can only be around four or five o'clock, they never call it 'afternoon tea' (ibid.). As regards 'sweet,' this word is only used freely as an adjective in upper-class English, but as a noun it is never used to refer to the sweet course at the end of a meal; 'pudding' is the right 'U' word, to be preferred to 'dessert,' too, because this is usually how upper-class people call the "selection of fresh fruit, served right at the end of a dinner, after the pudding, and eaten with a knife and a fork" (ibid.).

Apart from Fox's 'Seven Deadly Sins' (2004), among the words in Ross's long list (1959) there are a few more that are probably still rejected by the upper classes, such as 'greens,' 'perfume,' 'ill,' 'preserve,' 'wealthy,' to which they prefer respectively 'vegetables,' 'scent,' 'sick,' 'jam,' 'rich.' This was also more recently shared by etiquette expert William Hanson, who committed to the compilation of an updated 'U/non-U' wordlist (2017). After conducting some interviews with other experts and some upper-class people (e.g., Oxford Professor Simon Horobin, a few Oxford students, and Lord Fermoy, cousin to Lady Diana),[25] who all agreed in identifying the 'lavatory/toilet' dichotomy as the greatest divide between upper and middle classes, he published "the 2017 U and non-U list," reported in the following table:

---

23 Ross argued that the non-U 'serviette'/ U 'napkin' dichotomy is "perhaps the best known of all the linguistic class indicators of English" (1959, 19).

24 'Sitting-room' is a more modern alternative to Ross's 'hall' and 'dining room' as U alternatives to 'lounge' (ibid.). Fox says 'drawing-room' is also frequent in upper-class contexts, despite sounding slightly too pretentious, but definitely more accepted than 'living-room,' which is as non-U as 'lounge' (2004, 218–219).

25 Hanson's interviews are collected in a podcast on the website of BBC Radio 4: https://www.bbc.co.uk/programmes/b091w2p4 (last accessed 12/09/2020).

Table 4 – Revisited U/non-U list[a]

U words	non-U words
Alcohol	Booze
Antique / Old	Vintage
Avocado	Avo
Basement	Lower Ground
Champagne / Prosecco	Bubbly / Fizz
(I'm going for a) Coffee	(I'm going for a) Latte/Cappuccino/Flat White
Cooked Breakfast	Full English
Film	Movie
(I'm) Finished	(I'm) Done
Hello	Hey
Jam	Preserve
Lavatory / Loo	Toilet
Lunch (for the midday meal)	Dinner (for the midday meal)
May I have	Can I get
Napkin	Serviette
Phone	iPhone / Blackberry
Pudding	Sweet / Dessert
Pyjamas	PJs
Repartee	Banter
Sitting Room / Drawing Room	Lounge
Sofa	Settee / Couch
Takeaway	Deliveroo
Taxi	Uber
Toasted Sandwich	Toastie
(Do you...) Understand (me...)	(Do you...) Get (...me)
University	Uni
Wine	Vino

a https://www.bbc.co.uk/programmes/articles/3qF356d7d2D6h98CdCWxf8z/ten-words-that-prove-you-arent-posh (last accessed 12/09/2020).

From this 'U/non-U' revisited list, it can be inferred that more than having their own specific vocabulary, upper-class people are more conservative in their lexical choices and are particularly resistant to the use of brand names, abbreviations and American words. Also, they appear to be surprisingly reluctant to the use of some foreign borrowings, which are sometimes mistakenly considered as 'cultivated' and 'posh' choices.[26] However, Taggart provides a list of foreign words and expressions that "may take their place with pride in the Elegant vocabulary" (2010, 14–19); such words come especially from Latin (e.g., *ad hoc, per se, status quo, vice versa*, etc.) and French (e.g., *je ne sais quoi, laissez-faire, mot juste, savoir-faire*, etc.) (ibid.).

Both Fox (2004) and Hanson (2017) also argue that members of the upper classes are, contrarily to popular belief, much more direct than the middle classes, in the sense that they are not afraid to name controversial words or topics; euphemisms are usually avoided by the élite, who generally say, for example, 'die' and never 'pass away' (Hanson 2014, 14). Although there is no authorial evidence about it, it might even be suggested that swear words are not perceived as outrageous in upper-class contexts as people from the middle and lower classes might think. In Fox (2004), we read that "Jilly Cooper recalls overhearing her son telling a friend 'Mommy says that 'pardon' is a much worse word than 'fuck'' " (ibid., 211) and in the film *Educating Rita* (Gilbert 1983), as quoted in Ranzato (2018), the protagonist says "It's the aristocracy who swears the most. It's all 'Pass me the fucking pheasant,' with them" (ibid., 214). Naturally, these are not strong enough evidence to argue that the British upper classes make an extended use of swear words, but it might serve as a provocative starting point for a study on the use of taboo words in aristocratic contexts.

Despite not being an infallible indicator, it is worth mentioning that the upper-class children tend to call their parents 'Mummy' and 'Daddy,' while in lower-class contexts 'Mum' and 'Dad' are more frequent. Correspondingly, if an adult still uses 'Mummy/Daddy,' he/she is most probably upper-middle or above (Fox 2004, 223). 'Ma/Da,' as abbreviations of the French words 'mama/papa,' and the Latin 'mater/pater' were once used in aristocratic families, but they are now considered old-fashioned (Ross 1954, 29–30, quoted in Ranzato 2018, 218) and their use is restricted to historical representations of upper-class characters in cinema and television (see Chapter 4).

---

26 Neither the word 'cultivated' nor the word 'posh' are used by upper-class people (Ross 1959, 17–19; Fox 2004, 220).

In an article on *The New York Times Magazine*, Lohr (1992) observed that upper-class people have their own slang, building on some indications provided by John Simpson, at the time co-editor of *The Oxford English Dictionary*; for instance, the author writes, words like 'bumf' to refer to paper documents, 'brill' instead of 'brilliant,' and 'for yonks' as an alternative to 'for ages' are commonly heard in aristocratic contexts. He also adds that "for his part, Jonathan Green, editor of *The Dictionary of Contemporary Slang* (published by Pan Books Ltd.), sees juvenile nostalgia in upper-class expressions like crispies (for "money"), stiffies (for "party invitations") and wrinklies (for "older adults")." In the case of the Royalties specifically, Wales (1994, 7) points out that they are noted to use expressions which are "either left over from their prep- and public-school days (*thicko*; *weed*; *twit*; *nit*: all 'idiot'); or which are widely current in colloquial Estuary English: *for/in yonks* ('for ages'); *bog* ('lavatory'); *chuffed* ('very pleased')" (ibid.).

Apart from the words listed and commented so far, some others can also be mentioned as being perceived as being typical of an upper-class speech (perhaps a stereotypical one), like the way of addressing one's friends 'old chap/ old chum/ old bean/ old fruit/ old sport,' the expressions 'Jolly good!' (to show approval), 'Golly gosh/ Bugger/ Crickey' (to show surprise), 'Crumbs' (to show worry), 'Poppycock' (to say something is nonsense), and some adjectives like 'spiffing' and 'splendid' (to say something is great).[27]

1.4. Final discussion

Upper-class English is usually associated with Received Pronunciation (RP), and this first chapter started by pointing out that, although this is true, it must be clarified that there exist several forms of RP, and the one spoken by the upper classes is the Upper-crust RP, or U-RP (Wells 1992). Other names for the same accent are Conservative RP (Gimson 1970) and Conspicuous General British (Cruttenden 2014).

---

27 These expressions are taken from various Youtube videos by professional mother-tongue teachers of English as L2, such as *English with Lucy*, *Eat Sleep Dream English*, *Love English with Leila & Sabrah*.

U-RP is thus the spoken accent of the upper-class 'sociolect,' namely the variety at the top of the diastratic axis of the English language in UK. This is distinguished from 'style,' which is a diaphasic variation (Hernández-Campoy 2016, quoting previous authoritative studies); however, the distinctive linguistic features of this social-class dialect can also be adopted or emphasised in certain situations, since they constitute what can be considered as an example of 'enregistered speech style' (Agha 2007).

Chapter 1 was then dedicated to the delineation of a complete description of upper-class English in every linguistic aspect through the collection of sparse insights on the topic from both academic (Wells 1992 and 1998; Wales 1994; Harrington et al. 2000; Fabricius 2007; Ranzato 2018; Richards 2018) and non-academic literature (Mitford 1949; Ross 1959; Fox 2004; Taggart 2010; Hanson 2017). What resulted from this review is that the distinguishing features of the English spoken by upper-class people in Britain are:

- a general phenomenon of raising of vowel sounds;
- an occasional use of tapped /r/ and [ɪn] variant;
- a clear and emphatic articulation of some consonants, such as /t/;
- a distinctive position of the larynx ('plumminess');
- an occasional use of 'me' instead of 'my;'
- a tendency to make an abundant use of old-fashioned modals, like 'shall;'
- a firm rejection of some words, such as 'pardon' and 'toilet,' in favour of 'what/sorry' and 'lavatory/loo.'

While the phonological and prosodic characteristics are recognised as distinctive of the speech of upper-class people, as they are mentioned in scholarly literature, from the lexical point of view only a few arbitrary indications could be found during the research process. This means that a systematic sociolinguistic research on this topic is much needed, but the elements that were listed in this chapter may still be useful as a basis for the textual analysis of the following chapters. Through such analysis, it will also be possible to verify the frequency of the linguistic features mentioned in this chapter to identify which ones are real indicators or markers of upper-class English, or mere stereotyped characteristics that are now exclusively used in the representation of aristocratic people in the fictional dialogue.

Chapter 2   Past, present and future of upper-class English

2.1. A history of upper-class English

This chapter will be devoted to the attempt at delineating a diachronic evolution of the language of the upper classes in Britain, with the aim of providing an historical background to the present form and perception of this sociolect and its internal sociolinguistic variation; this historical excursus and description of the present status of upper-class English will lead to a final section dedicated to the prediction of the possible future evolution of this language variety.

Dealing with the history of a spoken language is, needless to say, an extremely complicated task, due to the lack of recordings of natural speeches and dialogues, at least up to a certain point, and even more complicated is to trace the diachronic evolution of the spoken language of a specific social class. Nevertheless, thanks to an attentive bibliographical study of some manuals on the history of English and insights in the field of historical sociolinguistics, sparse allusions to the language of the English aristocracy were traced and discussed in this chapter.

2.1.1. The 'Anglo-French' period

Following the traditional periodisation of the history of the English language, this section should start with the Old English period (the fifth to the eleventh centuries). However, there is not much information regarding the differences between the language of the lower class and the aristocracy at that time. We know that there were many different dialects, but, unfortunately, we do not know much about them because not many texts survived and it is impossible to know about the relationship between written and spoken usage of these Anglo-Saxon dialects (Leith 2005, 16–17). Latin was certainly considered as a 'high language' and we may assume that, since many texts were written in that language, its knowledge was a preferable skill among the nobles of the time, but it was probably used as a spoken language only in monasteries. It might be argued, then, that the Old English as we know it today from written texts reflects the language of the educated élite (ibid.).

After the Norman conquest, the Middle English phase (the twelfth to the fifteenth centuries) started. The new invaders brought their language, the variety of French spoken in Normandy, which did not replace English, but certainly influenced it. Most of the population in England, in fact, continued to speak their language, despite being in contact with a new one, which lived side by side to English. The Normans imposed as a ruling class, and their language spread inside the upper strata of the society, creating a situation of diglossia[28] (Nevalainen 2006, 29). This was further explained by Baugh and Cable as follows:

> For 200 years after the Norman conquest, French remained the language of ordinary intercourse among the upper classes in England. At first, those who spoke French were those of Norman origin, but soon through intermarriage and association with the ruling class numerous people of English extraction must have found it to their advantage to learn the new language, and before long the distinction between those who spoke French and those who spoke English was not ethnic but largely social (2013, 110).

Moreover, as argued by Leith (2005), French established as "the High language of law, government, administration, [...] courtly literature and religion" (ibid., 20) and, at least until the fourteenth century, it was spoken as L1 by the English monarchs (ibid., 22). Probably, some of them were even monolingual French speakers, and this was due to the fact that the English monarch was also the Duke of Normandy and had a close connection to the continent; the same can be applied to the nobility in general, who had possessions in the continent, and whose constant moving across The Channel played a crucial role in their continued use of French for many centuries. In other words, French was the most useful language for the social interests of the Anglo-French nobility, while English was considered as a socially inferior language, which is why members of the upper classes

---

28 The term 'diglossia' refers to the situation of coexistence of two different languages in a community: one is considered as prestigious, to be used in formal situations and in written texts, and one used primarily in informal contexts. It is, therefore, distinguished from 'bilingualism,' which is the coexistence of two linguistic codes equally prestigious.

did not feel the need to cultivate it, but this does not necessarily mean that they had no knowledge of it (Baugh and Cable 2013, 112–113). In fact, although the appearance of manuals for the teaching of French (more or less from 1250) and the conspicuous use of French in private and public letters makes evident that French was the official language of the court, English was spoken by the greater part of the population, so it is plausible to imply that many upper-class people acquired some familiarity with it (ibid., 116).

After the loss of Normandy (1204), French continued to be spoken by the English aristocracy for most of the thirteenth century because its knowledge had become a social marker in England, but also because it was obtaining a wide popularity in all civilised Europe (ibid., 128–129). However, the close political connection was lost together with the loss of lands on the continent, so that English aristocrats had no longer interests in France and, as a consequence, "the spread of English among the upper classes was making steady progress." (ibid., 131). By the year 1300, this progress had led to a renewed linguistic situation among upper classes: as argued by Baugh and Cable, children of the nobility were expected to speak French fluently, but their mother tongue was English (ibid., 132). The scholars supported their thesis by mentioning about a treatise to teach French written by Walter of Bibbesworth at the beginning of fourteenth century, where this language is clearly treated as an L2, given the presence of an English glossary and of a few comments on the importance of the acknowledgment of French by 'cultivated' people (ibid.). As Ingham puts it, at that time French simply remained as "the badge of ancestral superiority: tracing one's lineage to the Conqueror and his companions meant membership of an elite class" (2012, 32), but it was no longer the first language of noble children.

The decline of French as an L1 among the English aristocracy during the fourteenth century was also due to the fact that the French that was gaining popularity all over Europe was the variety spoken at the French court, which had developed into something quite different from the French spoken in Normandy and England, so that the latter was starting to be considered 'not-good' French (Leith 2005, 23–24; Baugh and Cable 2013, 135). This variety is, in fact, generally labelled as 'Anglo-French' or 'Anglo-Norman' to separate this insular evolution of the French spoken in Normandy from the Central French of Paris (Ingham 2012, 3–4).

What is important about the notion that the English aristocracy used to speak a form of French in the Middle Ages is that, naturally, they did not suddenly switch to English, and the process must have been slow and gradual. For this reason, but also for the popularity of continental French in the fourteenth century, as previously mentioned, upper-class people continued to use numerous French words. Thanks to the social prestige of the language of the élite, many of these words were introduced into the English language, and some of them are part of every-day language nowadays, such as 'pass,' 'join,' 'large,' 'chase,' etc. (Leith 2005, 24). More specifically, as Baugh and Cable affirm, the upper classes set a standard in more than one semantic field, such as fashion (the word 'fashion' itself was originally a French loanword), domestic and culinary life ('dinner' and 'supper' were French words, as well as the names of many items and food products), and social life (especially associated with activities like hunting and riding) (2013, 166–167).

2.1.2. The standardisation of the upper-class accent

It is often mentioned by scholars, and it will also be further explored later in this section, that "the upper ranks and professional people were instrumental in spreading new linguistic forms into the General dialect" (Nevalainen 2006, 139), but with the rise of the middle class and the consolidation of its power during the Early Modern period (the mid-sixteenth to the eighteenth centuries), several linguistic innovations came from "below the gentry" (ibid.). For example, the diffusion of the use of 'you' as a subject pronoun for the singular came from the middle class (ibid.).

Starting from this period, the East Midland variety began to circulate all over the country thanks to the movements of the London merchants. This dialect was possibly used as a sort of lingua franca, and this 'norm of communication' was not due to the prestige or the social power of the people who spoke it, but for its 'usefulness' for business (Leith 2005, 33). However, the power of the social élite also played a fundamental role in affirming the English spoken in the East Midland, because several sons of wealthy and noble families started to mix in the schools in Oxford and Cambridge (ibid.), whereas in their homes they probably spoke their local accents and they continued to do so at least until the eighteenth century, as argued by Görlach (1999, 28).

It is in the second half of the eighteenth century, which is usually identified as the beginning of the Late Modern Period, that some scholars started to feel the need for a standardised language to disseminate all over the country. This process was possible thanks to the formal teaching of the language according to a 'prescriptive' approach, which consisted in the evaluation of 'correct' variants and the stigmatisation of 'wrong' variants (Leith 2005, 42). By this time, the East-Midland dialect had spread even more and its use among the élite made it a prestigious accent; as a consequence, this variety was naturally selected as a base for what would become the Standard British English as we know it today. However, the work of grammarians and linguists of the time[29] only managed to provide a norm for the written language, while a standard pronunciation was harder to prescribe because even among the upper classes different accents were spoken, as it is also explained by Leith:

> Unfortunately for the codifiers, the usage of London in the early years of standardisation was extremely mixed. There was still considerable variation in pronunciation, for instance, amongst the upper class; what is more, such usage was constantly being pulled hither and thither by aristocratic fashion, educated pedantry, and the unmonitored speech of ordinary Londoners. But by the early nineteenth century, the recommendations of the codifiers could be embraced by those social classes who felt the need to mark their speech off from the class below (ibid.).

In the early nineteenth century, in fact, the aristocracy started to adopt a codified pronunciation,[30] which was taught in public schools and whose practice was closely controlled. Noble learners were the only privileged recipients of this prescribed spoken form, and the East-Midland accent thus became the upper-class accent (later named Received Pronunciation).

---

29 Some of the most influential figures of the 'age of prescriptivism' are, for instance, Samuel Johnson, who wrote his *Dictionary of the English Language* in 1755, and Robert Lowth, author of *Short Introduction to English Grammar* (1762).

30 The first dictionaries that dealt with the codification of the pronunciation were published by James Buchanan (1757), Thomas Sheridan (1790) and John Walker (1791).

This process is quite exceptional, since "in no other country in the world are pronunciation and social class so closely and clearly linked" (ibid., 47).

With the gradual identification of the upper-class language as the 'correct' language, some phonological phenomena came to stand as linguistic shibboleth, or, following Mugglestone's definition, "symbols of social divide" (2007). This is especially the case of H-dropping, as also explained in section 1.3. The clear pronunciation of /h/ in initial position was one of the rules of the codified standard language, and phonetician Thomas Sheridan provided some tips in his dictionaries and manuals on how to acquire this speech habit, but only the members of the upper-crust society had access to the higher education and to pronunciation guides (Tieken-Book van Ostade 2009, 24); consequently, /h/ became "an almost infallible test of education and refinement" (Sweet 1980, quoted in Mugglestone 2007, 95). Talking about aspiration, another sound that was considered as socially marked was [hw] for those words that start with the cluster 'wh-'; while /h/ is still today a linguistic symbol of politeness and education, [hw] was lost despite being used by upper-class speakers in the eighteenth century (Jones 2006, 109–110). The [ɪn] variant (see section 1.3) is another feature that was generally used by the élite in that period, and which is now adopted only by the older generation of U-RP speakers; this suggests that this form is closer to the 'original' prescribed standard, but it has lost prestige throughout the centuries, although it has not completely disappeared like [hw] (Milroy and Milroy 2002, 33). On the contrary, nowadays it can be widely heard in some regional accents and, although it is sometimes used to affect the language of upper-class characters in cinema and television (see Chapter 4), its "social evaluation [...] has altered" (ibid., 82). The command of these markers of speech, considered to be 'non-regional,' played a fundamental role in the social and cultural definitions of the 'lady' and the 'gentleman.' (Mugglestone 2007, 138).

2.1.3. Victorian upper-class English

After many decades of teaching and spreading of the linguistic standard among the upper classes, this variety became a well-established sociolect that the members of the high society learnt as an L1. Both the linguistic and social etiquette were taught to the noble children in their households, so that they naturally knew how to modulate their language according to the situations even before going to school. As argued by Görlach (1999, 38), during the Victorian age "the craze for correctness was a predominantly middle-class feature" and it was not rare for upper-class speakers to use non-standard features like 'ain't' and 'don't' for the third-person singular, although they were aware that such use had to be confined to the informal familiar speech only (ibid., quoting Denison 1998, 197). It was even proposed by Honey (1989, 44–46) that some stigmatised features were even cultivated in the aristocratic households as a reaction to the social threat from the middle classes.

Phillipps (1984), talking about the language of the aristocracy during the nineteenth century, also agrees that "it would be wrong [...] to equate upper-class English with grammatical correctness. There were, certainly, many grammars for Victorian ladies and gentlemen to read, but young gentlemen, at least, were usually too busy learning Latin" (ibid., 67). Apart from the contractions 'ain't' and 'don't' for all persons, it was not rare to hear speakers "of good standing" to use 'you was' (ibid., 68). The scholar used a corpus of private letters, documents and novels in which we find upper-class characters in order to provide a list of grammatical features of the Victorian upper-class English. Novels by such authors as Austen, Thackery, Trollope and Disraeli were particularly useful in this sense, because they contain several dialogues that represent the oral speech of noble characters, although, as Görlach (1999, 36) comments, these data "have to be interpreted with great caution." However, given the lack of other testimonies on the historical form of the upper-class sociolect, it is still interesting to briefly sum up some of the syntactical aspects proposed by Phillipps (1984, 70–78) as peculiar of the nineteenth-century upper-class speech:

- The use of present tense to express future, e.g. "Harriet Smith *marries* Robert Martin" (Jane Austen, *Emma*, ch. 54);
- The use of the Past Simple where now the Present Perfect is the norm, e.g. "I never *was* at his house" (Jane Austen, *Sense and Sensibility*, ch. 20);
- The use of the past of 'do' to construct the negative and interrogative forms of the verbal periphrasis 'used to' and 'ought to,' e.g. "You *did*

not used to like cards" (Jane Austen, *Persuasion*, ch. 22). This is now the norm, and perhaps upper-class usage has had a defining role, but purists in the nineteenth century objected it in favour of 'used not' and 'ought not.'

- The use of 'be to' meaning 'must,' e.g. "I *am not to* believe this message" (Anthony Trollope, *The Vicar of Bulhampton*, ch. 64);
- The use of adverbs to express a different meaning than the original one, like 'absolutely' to qualify the truth of a statement ("Was he *absolutely* in an Estern divan?" – Anthony Trollope, *The Warden*, ch. 6) or 'quite' with an intensive rather than a moderate sense ("I have gained him *quite* and he supports me in everything" – Benjamin Disraeli, Letters, II, p. 175).

Fictional works of the period also show evidence that even from the point of view of articulation, according to Phillipps (ibid., 35–42), Victorian upper-class speech was not more correct than the speech of the lower classes. In particular, the narrator in George Meredith's *The Ordeal of Richard Feverel* (1859) makes a few comments on the lack of fluidity in the speech of noble people, and the graphical representation of the utterances by his most effete upper-class characters show an abundance of hesitations and repetitions. Especially for gentlemen, fluidity was not a requirement in a familiar situation; on the contrary, a sort of 'casualness' was valued for men, while noble women had a tendency to speak with a quieter tone (ibid.).

Finally, the Victorian novel is also, and above all, an important source to study the language of the nineteenth century from the lexical point of view. In the case of upper-class English, Phillipps (ibid., 42–51) talks about the existence of a real slang, arguing that "when social climbers imagined that the speech of the upper classes was free from 'low' expressions, they were wrong" (ibid., 43, following Brook 1976). The upper-class slang originated in public schools, and it was generally used by young men who had the privilege to study at Oxford or Cambridge, but we might dare imply that they also used and spread some of the slang words in their familiar context and in other exclusive gathering occasions. Phillipps (ibid.), mainly on the basis of Thomas Hughes's book *Tom Brown at Oxford* (1861), mentions some colloquial upper-class words that were often heard at Oxbridge, such as 'sapping' (studying hard), 'aeger' ('sick' in Latin), 'claret' (spilt blood), 'laster' (man with stamina), 'to pluck' (to fail), 'to floor' (to accomplish a work). The use of 'fellow' to indicate male individuals was also wide-spread in colleges (ibid.), and it is probably one of those words whose usage has originated in public-school contexts but that has gradually entered the lexical repertoire of upper-class English, as the analysis in Chapters 3 and 4 will show. During the Victorian period, the word 'fellow' "carried a strong suggestion of casual comradeship" (ibid., 47) and a woman would not have dared to use it in public; slang in general was considered as a "guarded male prerogative" (ibid., 48), but its adoption by the ladies became gradually more tolerated too.

Phillipps (ibid., 57–64) also discusses a series of expressions that were considered characteristic of the upper-class speech and that, in his opinion, could still be recognised as shibboleths for the upper-class speaker at the time of his writing. This list builds mostly on Ross (1959), yet the scholar also provides a little appendix of "somewhat at random, certain words and phrases which carry a suggestion of upper-class usage" (ibid., 65). Some of his most salient points are summed up in the following short list:

- 'quantities' to indicate large amounts, e.g., "There were *quantities* of books" (Thomas Creevey, *The Creevey Papers*, p.240);
- 'capital,' an epithet that "carries a suggestion of accurate yet austere-sounding praise" (ibid., 65), e.g., "the *capital* pen of a sister author" (Jane Austen, *Northanger Abbey*, ch. 14);
- 'particular' to refer to a very attentive attitude, e.g., "Lord Lufton had been rather *particular* in his attentions" (Anthony Trollope, *Framley Parsonage*, ch. 11);
- 'civil' to refer to people of an inferior social status who show a courteous attitude towards upper-class people, e.g., Mr Harding in Trollope's *The Warden* (ch. 16) thinks "Was ever anything so *civil*?" when is offered a couple of magazines and an evening paper by a waiter.

Finally, it is worth mentioning a few upper-class habits to address people during the Victorian Age, since modes of address are still considered as important social markers. In the English language, in fact, personal pronouns bear no pragmatic meaning like in other European languages, and modes of address are the only tools to convey a sense of courtesy, respect or formality in a conversation. By the nineteenth century, the use of 'thou' and its separation in meaning with 'you' had already died out, and different degrees of intimacy were expressed by the combination of titles, names and surnames. As Görlach (1999, 41) points out, "the most formal kind of address was to use the title and second name," while the use of the Christian name was confined to the family. The bare surname was between formal and informal and it was generally used in school or, occasionally, among men; otherwise, it was generally adopted to address servants, who had to use in return 'my lord/ lady' or 'your grace.' Noble children called their parents 'mama/ ma/ mammy/ mother' and 'papa/ pa/ daddy/ father' (ibid.). These conversational social rules are found not only in the novels of Pre-Victorian and Victorian authors mentioned in this section, but also in audiovisual period dramas. One of the most complete representation is perhaps found, among other period dramas, in the TV series *Downton Abbey* (2010–2015) where familiar and formal conversations among aristocratic people, but also with servants, are shown (see Sandrelli 2016, which will also be further discussed in Chapter 4). It is true that *Downton Abbey* is set after the Victorian Age, but it is also true that the structure of the society during the pre-war Edwardian Era was quite similar, and it was only after the Great War that feelings for a social revolution started to arise in Britain. The lifestyle of the upper classes was seen as anachronistic, sometimes even by some upper-class members themselves, who started to work as professionals, and thus got in touch with middle-class and upper-middle-class peers. Moreover, in mid twentieth century, families from every social class were exposed to different kinds of mass media, which had a great impact on the language.

However, as it was explored in Chapter 1, the upper classes are generally rather resistant to linguistic innovations, and at least until the 1930s the aristocracy in Britain still used those phonological features that Wells (1992) included in the description of U-RP but which he defined as "old-fashioned." For example, the [ɪn] variant was still used by upper-class people of all ages and not only by the older generation, because their status had been "secure enough for it to remain unmoved" (Leith 2005, 114). Only a couple of decades later, Ross's indications (1954, 1959) on what could be considered linguistically as 'U' or 'non-U,' including the debate that they originated, proves that in the second half of the twentieth century a form of enregistered upper-class speech existed. The whole historical excursus, in fact, was to show that while the prestige of the language of the upper classes certainly played a fundamental role in the process of the imposition of a standard form, it was only taken as a 'base form;' in fact, 'upper-class' should not be taken as a full synonym of 'standard.'

2.2. Present-day upper-class English

In Chapter 1, a complete description of modern upper-class speech was provided by listing the main phonological, prosodic, morpho-syntactical and lexical features that define this sociolect today in Britain. In some cases, basing on previous scholarly studies, there was an attempt at identifying those features as actual markers or indicators of aristocratic English or as stereotyped peculiarities that no longer correspond to the real language variety, and the textual analysis of the next chapter will hopefully contribute to expand on that side. In the same chapter, the aspect of the diaphasic variation was also included, while the first section of the current chapter dealt with the diachronic evolution of the upper-class sociolect. To complete the overview, this section will be devoted to the internal diastratic and diatopic variation of the language of the élite in Britain today, as well as its perception and status in present-day society.

2.2.1. Age and gender variability

Providing an outline of the internal variability of a social class is not an easy task, especially when the availability of data from authentic speaker tests are scarce, as in the case of the upper-class speech. It was previously mentioned that this scarcity is due to the fact that securing collaboration from such speakers is challenging, but also to the fact that it has long been assumed in dialectological research that the language of the élite social group is not too different from the standard and, consequently, less suitable as a subject for sociolinguistic studies (Ranzato 2017; Britain 2017; Fabricius 2018). In other words, as Britain (2017, 289) points out, "elite or 'upper-class accents' are imagined as stable" because their connection with the standard dialect is generally considered straightforward. Nevertheless, "elite speakers' accents [...], unlike the model standards accents they are ideologically associated with, are highly variable" (ibid., 291).

The analysis of the idiolects of selected influential members of the upper class (see next chapters) will offer some innovative data on the variation of the élite speech according to the age and the sex of the speaker, but for now a few general tendencies as described in the sociolinguistic scholarly literature can be mentioned and applied to this case. Speaking about gender differentiation in language, for example, Trudgill argues (2000, 79–80) that it is originated from the assumption that language is a social phenomenon and it is thus related to social attitudes; men and women are associated with different social roles, therefore they are expected to adopt different social behaviours, which also include language. In the previous section, it was mentioned that both ladies and gentlemen belonging to the aristocracy in the eighteenth and the nineteenth centuries were expected to adopt a 'refined' language, but it was also discussed how this pressure was even higher for women, whereas men were allowed the use of a slang. As argued by Mugglestone (2007, 138), "the gentleman might be duly distinguished by his perfection in such matters; the lady, however, was apparently to excel still further if she was fully to satisfy her right to such an appellation." This tradition seems to apply still today in every strata of society, being women generally expected to maintain a higher level of adherence to social and linguistic norms, while the use of non-standard forms by men is usually less misjudged (Trudgill 2000, 72–73). As Trudgill notices, a certain degree of non-standardness in male speech might even be desirable:

> [...] working class speech, like certain other aspects of working-class culture in our society, seems to have connotation of or associations with masculinity, which may lead men to be more favourably disposed to nonstandard linguistic forms than women. This, in turn, may be because working-class speech is associated with the 'toughness' traditionally supposed to be characteristic of working-class life – and 'toughness' is quite widely considered to be a desirable masculine characteristic (ibid.).

Building on Trudgill's words, therefore, we may expect to hear in the speech of upper-class men some recent innovations of Mainstream RP (e.g. HAPPY-tensing) rather than a pure form of U-RP, if not even an occasional use of working-class features like H-dropping and T-glottaling.

T-glottaling, for example, is apparently found in the spontaneous speech of the young élite generation, as briefly mentioned by Britain (2017, 292), who refers to the empirical investigations by Fabricius (2000) and Badia

Barrera (2015). Both scholars analysed the speech of a group of private-school students and they observed that such phenomenon is indeed detected in their speech, not much in medial position, but rather in final position (Badia Barrera 2015, 207). However, both works do not "aim at a *class* analysis" (Britain 2017, 293), but they focus on the spread of a single phonological phenomenon, concluding that T-glottaling "has to some extent lost its stigma, but not yet acquired prestige" (Fabricius 2000, 145). Badia Barrera (2015) compared the results from the analysis of speech of students from different types of private schools, both boarding and non-boarding schools, with the results obtained from a comprehensive one, and she observed that "RP informants from the school with highest social profile (private boarding) are considerably resisting T-glottaling in both word-medial and word-final contexts" (ibid., 206). This conclusion means that, although the new 'financialised' élite is a diverse group and families with various social backgrounds can afford to send their children to high fee-paying private school nowadays (Britain 2017, 295), an aristocratic élite is still recognisable. The younger generation of this circumscribed group has inevitably a more 'modern' speech, closer to Mainstream RP, which means that, due to the contact with other social-class peers and the influence of the media,[31] they are likely to use lower vowel sounds compared to those found in their grandparents' speech and they certainly do not use, for example, tapped-R (see section 1.3); yet, they are also far from using those features whose intrusion in RP is still not to be considered well established. To describe the difference in language between generations of upper-class people, we can resort to Gimson's distinction between Conservative RP and Advanced RP (1970, 88 – see section 1.1). Both forms correspond to Wells's U-RP (1992) and are 'heightened' versions of the central tendency that Gimson calls General RP ('mainstream,' for Wells), but while the former is associated with the older generation and reflects the stereotypical 'gentry aesthetics' (Britain 2017), the latter is spoken by the younger generation.

---

31 Badia Barrera (2015) noted non-trivial levels of American and Australian influences, like the intervocalic T-flapping, in the speech of boarding private-school attenders.

2.2.2. Regionalised upper-class English

Despite the fact that both Standard English and Received Pronunciation, which are the base of upper-class English, originated from the South-East of England (see section 2.1), they are now considered as non-regional forms. The defining characteristic of RP, in particular, is its "non-localisability within England" (Wells 1998, 14), and RP speakers are labelled as 'accentless' because RP is generally associated with the upper classes and traditionally "any regional accent is by definition not an upper-class accent" (Wells 1998, 14). Although it is hard to believe that a speaker never shows occasional 'hints' of regionality, it is true that the upper-class social group is generally highly self-conscious and its members are particularly attentive in the way they talk to reaffirm their social belonging (see the definition of 'social network' in section 1.2). Also, their residences are concentrated in the area of the Home Counties (Savage et al. 2013, 234), and, as Trudgill explains (2008, 3), RP is still to be considered typologically very close to the South-Eastern regiolect. Some features are slowly spreading into RP from below, but "there is selectivity. Although innovations spread into RP from lower-status accents, by no means all innovations do so" (ibid., 5), because this accent tends to retain its clear social distinctiveness (ibid.). In the case of the 'upper-crust' group of RP speakers, the lack of regional influences is even more generalised in all parts of England, because the upper-class society is characterised by the establishing of contacts over long distances too (Milroy and Milroy 1999, 49).

Received Pronunciation is undoubtedly a 'regionless' accent, but it is by all means an English accent; yet, different scholars (Trudgill 2008, Britain 2017, among others) have pointed out that it is often more generally associated to Britain in general, although this is not entirely correct, as Wells explains:

> [...] it is to be noted that all labels for accents in England tend to have social connotations as well as (except for RP) regional ones.
>
> We may extend this model to cover Wales as well as England without serious modification. But we cannot extend it to Scotland or Ireland, or of course to outside the British Isles. In Scotland and Ireland RP is generally seen as a foreign (English) accent; these countries have their own higher-class accents which differ in many important respects from RP (1998, 15)

Ireland is rather homogeneous in terms of social class, because the island was dominated by the English crown very early and the aristocrats living there were mostly British. It is true, however, that RP is not considered as a standard accent in Ireland, where the educated people speak Supraregional Southern Irish English in the Republic of Ireland (Hickey 2012) and South Ulster English in Northern Ireland (McCafferty 2007), but they are classified as standard middle-class accents and they do not have an 'upper' version.

In the case of Scotland, instead, despite the fact that it is still part of the UK, unlike Ireland, we can refer to the existence of a local upper class, because the Scottish crown was not dominated by the English one, but they were merely unified.[32] Consequently, Scotland had a court and an established Scottish nobility in the country, acquiring a specific linguistic variety. As it happens with RP in England, upper-class English in Scotland is also based on the standard accent, which is called Scottish Standard English and which is "prestigious in a way that a local English accent is not" (Wells 1992, 393), but it curiously shares some features with U-RP. This is perhaps due to the fact that with the union of the English and the Scottish crowns the members of the aristocracy of the two countries inevitably came into contact and developed a shared set of linguistic habits that defined their privileged social status. Aitken (1984) refers that this hybrid accent can be considered as an RP-accented variety, a sort of compromise between the most conservative version of Educated Scottish Standard English and RP; nevertheless, Aitken clarifies that is not a casual imitation of RP, but it is fully established and institutionalised:

> RP-accented English (often, it is true, accompanied by a few stylistic overt Scotticisms) is, without exception, the speech of all members of the hereditary landed gentry of Scotland, the lairds and clan chiefs and of the Scottish member of the royal family, the Queen Mother, since these persons have from the eighteenth century and earlier been accustomed to educate their children in expensive English private schools (the so-called 'Public Schools') or the few similar

---

32 Scotland became official part of the United Kingdom in 1707 with the Act of Union, but all the countries in the British Isles had been sharing the same sovereign since 1603, when James I Stuart, King of Scotland, succeeded the last English monarch, Elizabeth I Tudor.

establishments in Scotland, and have, since the seventeenth century, mixed (and intermarried) with the same social caste in England (ibid., 529).

To give a better understanding of the context where such a hybrid accent might be heard in Scotland, Aitken mentions (ibid.) the exclusive college for girls described in Muriel Spark's novel *The Prime of Miss Jean Brodie* (1961).

Following this indication, it is interesting to discuss briefly how this RP-accented English was rendered in the 1969 film adaptation of Spark's book, directed by Ronald Neame (Valleriani 2019).[33] The protagonist of the story is Miss Jean Brodie, played by Maggie Smith,[34] who is a teacher at the exclusive school Marcia Blaine in Edinburgh. In the film, she speaks with a sophisticated upper-class accent with some local features, which will be briefly mentioned in reference to the following short excerpt:

MISS BRODIE

Little girls, I'm in the business of putting old heads on young shoulders and all my pupils are the *crème de la crème.*

Give me a girl at an impressionable age and she is mine for a life. You girls are my **vocation.** If I had to receive a proposal of marriage tomorrow, from the Lord Lyon, King or Arms, I would decline it.

I'm dedicated to you in my prime... and my summer in Italy has convinced me that I am truly in my prime.

(*The Prime of Miss Jean Brodie*, 1969, min. 6:57)

The phonological features that would need discussion are in bold in the transcription, to draw the attention on what can only be noted acoustically. In particular, although Jean Brodie's accent is unquestionably a Scottish accent, she makes an abundant use of some peculiarities of U-RP, like the use of [ɪ] at the end of 'Italy' and 'truly,' and the rounding of the lips to

---

33 I have discussed on this topic, and in particular on the translation strategies that were adopted in the Italian adaptation to render this accented upper-class English, at the international conference *Media for All 8 – Complex Understandings*, which took place at Stockholm University in June 2019. See the abstract at the following link: https://www.tolk.su.se/english/media-for-all-8/programme/abstracts/translating-regionalised-upper-class-english-1.428547 (last accessed 10/10/2020).

34 For this part, Smith won an Academy Award for Best Actress in 1970. She simulated again a Scottish upper-class accent in the *Harry Potter* saga (2001–2011), where she played the role of Professor Minerva McGonagall.

produce the affricate sound in the suffix '-tion' (e.g. in 'vocation'). Rhoticity, as it was discussed in Chapter 1, is another traditional 'U' feature, but it is shared with Educated Scottish Standard English; the only difference is that, in U-RP, tapped-R [ɾ] is heard only occasionally in the within-word environment (e.g. 'marriage,' 'tomorrow,' 'prime' in the excerpt), while in Scottish the 'r' is rhotic in all environments, including in final position (in this case it is generally a retroflex approximant, e.g. 'for' in the excerpt) (Wells 1992, 411). Vowel sounds are generally shorter and closer than in RP throughout the whole film, this being one characteristics of Scottish English, but the TRAP vowel is often realised as in 'U' speech. An instance is to be found at minute 19:40, where one of Miss Brody's pupils, Sandy, emphasises a remarkably open and long sound in the word 'that': "I don't think they did anything like that [ðɛæt]. Their love was above all that [ðɛæt]." Also, both Miss Brodie's and Sandy's prosody is very high-pitched, and the former's voice quality is slightly 'plummy.'

It must be clarified that the linguistic indications about the hybrid Scottish/U-RP accent that are found in the film adaptation of *The Prime of Miss Jean Brodie* refer to the fictional rendition and not the actual speech of upper-class people in Scotland, but its concise analysis served to argue that when we deal with upper-class English in Britain it is true that it is subject to a scarce diatopic variability, but it is also true that the Scottish area should be considered as an exception.

2.2.3. The perception of upper-class English

Few people in Britain have ever met a genuine working cowboy: but we have our stereotyped view of what a cowboy is like. We know what he wears, the way he behaves, the kind of food he is likely to eat, and the way he talks. And if we came across someone dressed as a cowboy, hitching his horse to the wooden rail outside the saloon, then swaggering in and up to the bar to order a whiskey in a U-RP accent, we should notice that something was odd. Accents constitute an important part of many stereotypes (Wells 1998, 29).

With this funny image, Wells introduces the topic of the relationship between language and stereotypes, arguing that the accent of the speaker is part of the indexical information that the listener uses to classify him/her into an appropriate stereotype (ibid.). For example, the scholar, quoting Giles (1970 and 1971), reports that RP speakers are usually considered to be more ambitious, smarter, more self-confident and more hard-working than the speakers of regional accents, but they are also regarded as less sociable, less good-natured and with less sense of humour (ibid., 30). RP has always been the accent of a minority, despite the plans that BBC initially implemented to establish it as a reference accent, but television certainly made a huge contribution in letting people all over the UK 'receive' it, as its name suggests. In this way, an image of the RP speaker was projected in the country, which started as an image of prestige, an image that some part of the population aspired to acquire, but, along with the socio-cultural revolutions and the class-struggle movements of the second half of the twentieth century, RP gradually became the symbol of an imposed model that had to be rejected. Consequently, negative attitudes towards the RP speaker arose and regional accents, on the contrary, found their space in television, especially in films and TV series, but partly in broadcasting too (Valleriani 2021a, 196-199). Trudgill (2008, 1–2) argues that RP is no longer a "necessary passport" for professional jobs, and nowadays some regional accents are apparently considered more effective when the aim is to appear customer-friendly; for instance, Di Martino (2019, 73) highlights that Geordie is one of the accents that has recently been best evaluated in surveys on call centre trends.[35] In other words, "RP accent can be more of a disadvantage in certain situations than was formally the case" (Trudgill 2008, 1–2).

The sociolinguistic research of the 1980s has accordingly pointed out that RP was considered as the accent of "insincere" and "distant" people, whereas regional accents like that of the Yorkshire area and that of the city of Edinburgh received a much more positive evaluation (Ranzato 2017, 18, quoting Crystal 2010, 27). RP has consequently become even more than ever a synonym of elitism, it sounds 'posh' and 'snob' and it is generally

---

35 The case of Geordie was explored extendedly by Di Martino (2019), who pointed out that "the representation of Geordie in advertising did not simply appear to have improved, but to have totally changed its position in the power distribution network of British varieties, shifting – with its presence in the voice-over of an advert – from constituting a counter-hegemonic force in the linguistic landscape of TV programming to becoming itself a symbol of conservative, hegemonic linguistic ideology. Indeed, a Royal Navy TV advert spurred a harsh debate over the choice to dub a Cumbrian Navy sailor's voice with a Geordie accent (Seddon 2016)" (ibid., 86–87).

disliked by the population (ibid., 23, quoting Cheshire and Edwards 1993, 42 and 46), because "a posh voice is seen as naff and unfashionable" (ibid., quoting Morrish 1999).

In the specific case of U-RP there are no reaction studies, but it can be surely assimilated to what has been previously quoted about RP in general; also, building on the concept that listeners tend to evaluate language varieties into 'good and bad' (Preston 2002; Trousdale 2010), it can be assumed, following Richards (2010), that "for example, NBE [Northern British English] speakers might evaluate U-RP as bad because they think that it sounds exaggerated [...]" (ibid., 53). A little more can perhaps be inferred by the use of this accent in the fictional dialogue. The topic will be further explored in Chapter 4, but for now it is worth mentioning that even from anecdotal evidence it can be noticed that fictional characters in recent audiovisual productions share a set of traits that show how this particular variant of RP is perceived. In particular, U-RP speakers are depicted as being astute, cunning, witty and humorous in a cynical way, but also cold, selfish and unscrupulous. The characterisation of the British Villain with an RP voice has quite a long tradition in the history of the Anglophone cinema (see Chapter 4), and this linguistic rendition has recently become even more accurate: evil characters are not simply RP speakers, but they often use a few stereotypical upper-class features. As it was mentioned, a whole chapter will be dedicated to the upper-class language in audiovisual productions, but a small example taken from a theatre representation is offered here to give a clearer idea on how an aristocratic accent is perceived. *Hamilton* (2015) is a musical written by Lin-Manuel Miranda, based on the life of the American statesman Alexander Hamilton. The character of King George III in the musical embodies the English enemy. He sings three songs during the play, and one of these, *You'll Be Back*, ends with the following lines:

> "*When you're gone, I'll go mad*
> *So don't throw away this thing we had*
> *'Cause when push comes to shove*
> *I will kill your friends and family... to remind you of my love.*"

> (*Hamilton*, min. 22:45 on Disney+)[36]

---

36 The streaming version on Disney+ is a montage of recorded scenes taken from different representations that took place in New York in 2016.

Actor Jonathan Groff[37] adopts features like the mid vowels in TRAP and HAPPY words and makes an abundant use of tapped-R in all of his appearances on stage, and in these lines they are remarkably emphasised, specifically in the words 'mad' [mɜːd], 'friends' [frɜːndz], 'family' [fɜːmlɜː], 'remind' [ɹɪmaɪnd]. The U-RP accent used by Groff in *Hamilton* is not only stereotypical, but it is also stereotyped,[38] but it certainly gives the idea of how this kind of speech is perceived by the musical production, reflecting the existence of a real British upper-class *trope* in performative productions, even out of the UK.

2.3. Future perspectives

It is extremely hard to foresee the future of a language variety, especially when even its present-day aspects have been very rarely the focus of the scholars' "dialectological gaze" (Britain 2017, 289), like in the case of the upper-class sociolect. However, some hypotheses can be formulated based on what has been argued on the future of Standard English and Received Pronunciation.

As pointed out by Kerswill (2007, 49–50) the evolution of Standard English and RP relates to the phenomenon of dialect levelling, "by which differences between local accents/dialects are reduced, features which make them distinctive disappear and new features develop and are adopted by speakers over a wide area" (ibid.). Estuary English,[39] for example, was born thanks

---

37 Groff is only one of the several actors who played the role of George III in the musical, but his interpretation is one of the most memorable, especially because he appears in the recorded version.

38 The words 'stereotypical' and 'stereotyped' might be assumed as being synonyms, but they are in fact to be intended as two distinct processes: the use of a language variety in fictional dialogue is most probably part of character stereotyping, but that does not necessarily mean that the language variety is rendered in stereotyped way. As argued by Hodson (2014, 79), it is possible to find a character in a film who is made have a stereotypical accent according to his/her socio-cultural identity, while the portrayal of his/her accent may be perfectly accurate.

39 The term 'Estuary English' was proposed by Rosewarne (1984) because it refers to the regional variety spoken in the area along the River Thames and its estuary. Cruttenden (2014, 81–82), however, proposed the use of the alternative label 'London Regional General British.' Apart from Rosewarne (1984 and 1994) and the other scholars mentioned in the main section, see also Coggle 1993 and

to a regional levelling process (ibid., also confirmed by Przedlacka 2002 and Altendorf 2003), placing itself as "a middle ground" between RP and London Speech, or, in other words, "between Cockney and the Queen" (Rosewarne 1994, 3). In short, it can be considered as an accent convergence adopted by RP speakers who accommodate 'downwards' and local-accent speakers who accommodate 'upword.' (ibid., 7). Rosewarne does not exclude that Estuary English will become the RP of the future (ibid., 8, later argued by Altendorf 2003 too) and Wells (1994 and 1997) noticed a process of "Cockneyfication" that might result into permanent changes in the 'regionless' accent. This process includes a series of changes 'from below' in RP, some of which are now considered well established, such as Happy-tensing, the lowering of the TRAP vowel, L-vocalisation and T-glottaling (Kerswill 2007, 49; Trudgill 2008, 6–9), but the concept of dialect levelling is questioned by Trudgill (2008, 5), who affirms that "by the time RP reaches the level achieved by regional accents in a particular change today, the regional accents will have moved on even further, and the difference will remain."

Basing on Trudgill's words (ibid.), it might be thus assumed that Mainstream RP will gradually become closer and closer to Estuary English, while U-RP will be 'democratised' into Mainstream RP. To put it short, the upper-middle class may soon speak almost exclusively Estuary English, while what is now known as Mainstream RP may be the general speech of the upper classes. Arguably, RP will remain a 'regionless' accent, but it will probably be considered a social-class accent even more than today. This kind of process is certainly related to the phenomenon of dialect levelling, but in the case of RP speakers a feeling of "maintenance of distinctiveness" (ibid.)[40] must also be taken into account.

Nevertheless, the power of the media, and in particular of cinema and television, should not be underestimated. It was previously mentioned, and it will be widely discussed later in this volume, that the upper-class *trope* is often portrayed in film and TV productions, and the linguistic rendition of popular upper-class characters might influence the viewer's language.

De Pascale 2013 for a complete discussion on the aspects of this linguistic phenomenon.

40 The accent retain for social distinctiveness is related to sociolinguistic concepts that were discussed in section 1.2., e.g., social network theory.

Particularly for children, it is not rare to acquire some linguistic features to mimic the characters of the shows they like, even when they do not have familiarity with them in their everyday-life. For example, in 2019 some newspapers collected comments from American parents who noticed how their children were starting to utter some words with a 'Queen's' pronunciation[41] after watching *Peppa Pig* (2004–present) on television (*The Independent* 2019; *The Guardian* 2019). Linguists declared that it was exaggerated to associate these occurrences to a real accent development (ibid.), but it gives the idea on how linguistic rendition in the audiovisual dialogue can have a concrete impact on natural face-to-face language.

2.4. Final discussion

Chapter 2 completed the overview on upper-class English that was provided in Chapter 1 by discussing the language variety through a diachronic, diastratic and diatopic perspective.

A first testified linguistic separation between the lower and the upper classes dates back to the Middle Ages, after the Norman Conquest (1066), when the English nobility started to use French (or, better, Anglo-French) as a first language. During the Renaissance a certain level of knowledge of French was an expected skill for the members of the aristocracy, but by that time English had fully established as an L1 for them too. They used their regiolect like the rest of the population, but the East Midland dialect was starting to be adopted by noble people all over England, due to the tradition of receiving an education at Oxbridge colleges. This language variety was the one which was selected to be prescribed as a 'correct' standard during the eighteenth century, and members of the élite were the main recipient of grammar manuals and dictionaries. During the nineteenth century, middle-class people became more concerned in following the prescriptions of grammarians, while the aristocracy developed a slang and acquired nonstandard linguistic habits, which they continued to use as social markers of distinctiveness in the twentieth century, too. This historical outline of

---

41 Characters in the animated series *Peppa Pig* (2004–present) generally speak Mainstream RP, but, curiously, in episode 4x27 the protagonists pay visit to Queen Elizabeth, who is rendered with an extremely accurate upper-crust RP.

upper-class English showed how some popular preconceptions about this sociolect are not entirely true; first of all, although it is fundamentally a variant of Standard English and Received Pronunciation, upper-class English should not be considered as a model of correctness, since it has got its level of non-standardness, and secondly, the aristocrats are generally associated with French for historical reasons, but this does not necessarily mean that they use French loans in their everyday language more than people from other social strata.

Today upper-class English appears to be rather homogeneous, due to a strong sense of social distinctiveness, but it is subject to a certain degree of variability as it happens with every linguistic system. In particular, coherently to the principles of Variationist Sociolinguistics, the older generations appear to be more conservative than the younger generations, who speak a more modern version of U-RP, perhaps closer to Mainstream RP, and men are more likely to resort to a non-standard variant compared to women, who generally tend to adhere to the norm more closely. Even from the geographical point of view, upper-class English is characterised by a general homogeneity all over the UK, with the exception of Scotland, where an accented form of U-RP is used.

In the future, we might expect to find more innovations 'from below,' according to the process of dialect levelling, but we can assume that a certain degree of separation between the speech of the élite and that of the rest of the society will be retained.

Chapter 3   Upper-class English in real life: The Royal Family

3.1. The 'Queen's English'

'Queen's English' is, together with 'BBC English,' one of the alternative names given to Received Pronunciation in non-scholarly literature. The *Cambridge Advanced Learner's Dictionary and Thesaurus* defines it as "the English language as it is spoken in the south of England, considered by some people as a standard of good English,"[42] thus implying that the language of the Queen is the emblem of this spoken variety. However, it was pointed out in the previous chapters that it is certainly a fact that the English nobility and the Royal Family speak RP, but they speak a 'heightened' version of it that can be called U-RP, following Wells's terminology (1992).

In this section, on the other hand, 'Queen's English' is used to designate the authentic language of Queen Elizabeth II, which will be examined through the analysis of some transcriptions of Her Majesty's conversations taken from documentaries and interviews, and these results will be compared to previous studies on the topic. The chapter will then follow with the discussion of data from the analysis of the idiolect of some of the other members of the Royal Family, but also of other well-known figures of the English nobility, in order to provide a wider spectrum. The analysis will be conducted according to the principles of Sociophonetics (Thomas 2013) and Conversation Analysis (Sidnell 2009 and 2016).

*

Not many researchers focused on the language of the Queen, at least not until the 2000s, when a group of scholars conducted an acoustic analysis of nine Christmas broadcasts made by the Queen between 1952 and 1988. Harrington et al. (2000), in their research, concentrated on vowel change, being particularly concerned with stressed monophtongs, and they

---

42 https://dictionary.cambridge.org/it/dizionario/inglese/queen-s-english (last accessed 30/10/2020).

compared their results with speech formant data from 1980's Standard Southern British speakers taken from the MARSEC database[43] (Roach at al. 1994). The scholars discussed their results as follows:

> The acoustic analysis of these Christmas broadcasts shows that there has been a 'vertical' expansion of the vowel space from the 1950's to the 1980's and, to a lesser extent, a 'horizontal' compression. The vertical expansion is due to an F1[44] raising of the open vowels [ɑ ʌ æ ɒ], which suggests that they are phonetically more open in the 1980's than in the 1950's broadcasts, and an F1 lowering of all the other vowels, in particular [ɪ ʊ ɔ] (ibid., 73).
>
> [...]
>
> The conclusion that can be drawn from these results is that changes in the Queen's vowels between the 1950's and 1980's have been in the direction of a more mainstream RP. If this theory is correct, and if the vowel positions have continued to change beyond the 1980's, then the present-day Queen's vowel positions might have shifted even further in the direction of a vertical expansion and horizontal compression (ibid., 74).

However, although a change towards mainstream RP was noticed, the scholars also pointed out that throughout the whole material some features of U-RP were also heard, and apparently they did not lose frequency, such as tapped-R in intervocalic position, a 'back' /u/ and the use of [ɔ] instead of /ɒ/ in words like 'lost' (ibid, 65). In their article, they also suggest a few explanations for this change in the Queen's spoken language: apart from the physiological process of aging, Harrington et al (2000, 75) argue that the Queen might have adjusted to the broadcasting format, and she might have learnt how to deliver a clearer message. This process translated into an hyperarticulation effect in later broadcasts (ibid.).

Harrington (2005) later expanded the study with a new acoustic analysis of the Queen's Christmas broadcasts, this time focusing on the phenomenon of Happy-tensing. The result of this research was that the Queen's /ɪ/ has been going through the process of 'tensing,' but only with respect to the

---

43 The acronym refers to the 'Machine Readable Spoken English Corpus,' containing materials of various kinds in the 1980s.
44 According to Thomas's explanations (2013, 110), "the frequency of the first formant (F1) is correlated inversely with the height of the vowel" and "the frequency of the second formant (F2) is correlated directly with how front a vowel is."

first formant and not the second (ibid., 454). In other words, only a raising could be noticed, but not a fronting of the HAPPY vowel, because while the former is socially unmarked, the latter is a marker of Estuary English (ibid., quoting Wells 1997b). Harrington (2005) also added that "more casual variants in later broadcasts implies a certain degree of volition or intention i.e., that the sound changes are implemented by the Queen for a specific purpose (of sounding less formal, less aristocratic, more approachable, and so on)" (ibid., 453).

The results from these studies on the 'democratisation' of the Queen's spoken language, which are part of the wider research field of the evolution of RP (see, for example, Kerswill 2007, Fabricius 2007, Trudgill 2008), have recently been confirmed by Richards (2018), who also associated the changes in Elizabeth II's speech to a process of accommodation to her audience "to gain a higher level of acceptance from them in a bid to improve her popularity" (ibid., 52). The scholar's acoustic analysis took into considerations the broadcasts of the 1990s, too, and she tried to find a correlation between the Queen's vowel change and the popularity of the British monarchy. She noticed that the TRAP and STRUT vowels became more similar to Standard Southern British between 1997 and 1998, when the popularity of the monarchy had decreased (ibid., 63). That period corresponds to the aftermath of the death of the Princess of Wales, Diana Spencer, but, although the study concludes that in that time lapse the Queen's speech became less U-RP than the previous decades, it cannot be confirmed that this phenomenon is a direct consequence of the tragic event (ibid., 64). Richards (ibid.) argues, instead, that the fact that the Queen's style "varies more in 1999 compared to the preceding four years is interesting as the popularity of the British Monarchy increased at this time, and could be linked to an increase in the Queen's confidence."

The Queen's Christmas broadcasts constitute an invaluable acoustic corpus for linguistic investigations through a diachronic perspective, because they are among the very few recordings of the same person reproducing a similar content in similar circumstances (Harrington at al. 2000, 64). For instance, most of the broadcasts end with a fixed sentence, generally a construction like "and so I wish you all a very happy Christmas," which provides for several phonological elements to discuss and to compare. If we take as an example the same sentence as uttered in the broadcast recorded in

2019 (min. 5:38),[45] it can be noticed that, while the U-RP tapped-R in 'very' is retained, the vowels in 'happy' have lost their aristocratic 'openness,' i.e. [hæpiː]. However, the final sound in HAPPY words is still remarkably open in other contexts, for example when the Queen says previously in the same speech: "Prince Philip and I have been delighted to welcome our eighth great-grandchild into our *family* [fɜːmɪlɪ]" (min. 3:55).

Conducting an acoustic analysis of the Christmas broadcasts of the years 2000s and 2010s would certainly be interesting and it would offer a valuable expansion to the studies by Harrington et al. (2000), Harrington (2005) and Richards (2018); yet, other types of recording were selected as case studies in this chapter, forasmuch as the scope of this research is to compare upper-class English in 'natural' dialogue with its representation in the audiovisual dialogue. For this reason, the conversational format was preferred, since it corresponds to what Labov (2006) calls 'Casual Style,' the most natural and spontaneous speech. While in this style the attention of the speaker is not focused on the way he/she pronounces words, in speeches like the Christmas broadcasts, which Labov (2006) would label as 'Passage Reading Style,' the speaker's self-monitoring is higher, and this might determine a lower level of authenticity and a more conscious avoidance of socially-marked linguistic features (Hernández-Campoy 2016, 78). The first Christmas broadcast (1957) will nonetheless be part of the analysis in Chapter 5, where some famous speeches by the Queen will be compared to their represented version in the TV series *The Crown*.

In order to give an outline of the way Elizabeth II speaks in informal situations, the following documentaries were examined:

- *Monarchy: The Royal Family at Work*, 5 episodes, 60'–90', BBC, 2007, directed by Matt Reid;
- *The Coronation*, 60', BBC, 2018, directed by Harvey Lilley.

Both documentaries feature conversations between the Queen and interviewers or secretaries. Admittedly, the only recorded material that contains real live every-day situations of the Royal members is *Royal Family*, filmed in 1969 and directed by Richard Cawston, but it is currently

---

45 The Queen's Christmas broadcast 2019 can be viewed at https://www.youtube.com/watch?v=KgvZnxNAThM&t=348s (last accessed 30/10/2020).

unavailable. This documentary was commissioned to celebrate Prince Charles's investiture as Prince of Wales (Bastin 2009, 38), and the idea about a filmed documentary was especially welcomed by Prince Philip, who thought that it would offer an original humanised view of the Royal Family that would increase the popularity of the monarchy (Meares 2019). The documentary was a success in terms of number of views, but most of the critics agreed on the fact that "the mystique of the royalty had been compromised" (Rieden 2019). The Queen probably felt the same, and, as a consequence, "Buckingham Palace locked the film in the royal archives never to be seen in its entirety again without Her Majesty's permission" (ibid.).[46] In fact, it was aired on television only once again, in 1977, and a small video clip of 90" was shown at London's National Portrait Gallery in 2011 (ibid.). The same video clip can still be viewed on the internet, so a couple of linguistic aspects can be mentioned, but no transcript will be provided in this context, due to copyright issues.[47] The most striking aspect of this short footage available online is the prosody of the Royal Family, which sounds extremely high-pitched, especially Elizabeth's intonation, and from the phonological point of view almost all the features listed by Wells (1992, 280–283) can be detected (see Chapter 1). Tapped-R and the open vowels in HAPPY, TRAP and CLOTH words are especially audible. Moreover, an abundant use of emphasising adjectives and adverbs (e.g., 'extremely,' 'extraordinary' and 'terribly') is clearly evident.

In the other two documentaries, on the other hand, a few more mainstream-RP features can be heard, but the spoken language of the Queen still sounds aristocratic on the whole. *Monarchy: The Royal Family*

---

46 The episode 3x04 of *The Crown* is dedicated to the difficulty of the Royal Family in adjusting to the filming process in Buckingham Palace. The episode also shows the controversy that this initiative created inside and outside the palace.

47 It was possible in the past to submit a formal request to the BBC to watch the documentary for research purpose, and it was my intention to do the same and try and include it in the corpus for the analysis of this chapter. However, the sanitary emergency of 2020 made it complicated to plan a research period in the UK. The linguistic analysis of *BBC Royal Family* (1969) would probably offer interesting results to expand this study on upper-class English in the natural dialogue, and it thus constitutes a possible future step in this research.

at Work, filmed in 2007, is defined as a 'fly-on-the-wall' documentary,[48] and it follows the British Royal Family over the course of one year. Each of the five episodes follow some of the main institutional events that Queen Elizabeth and other members of the Royal Family had to attend in 2007. The whole series covers about six hours of voice-over narration, interviews with people who work daily in the Palace, and some short excerpts of conversation between the Queen and her employees and some prominent figures like Tony Blair, Prime Minister at the time of the filming. In particular, in episode 1, entitled *The State Visit*, Blair visits the Queen to discuss her forthcoming state visit to the US, and she mentions a reception she has hosted for American expatriates in London. Part of the conversation is transcribed below:[49]

– Scene 1:

TONY BLAIR	You had a reception here for the Americans in London.
QUEEN ELIZABETH	Yesterday, yeah -- Most of them had never met each other before and, uh -- they're all very very busy here. Apart from students, there are a lot of business people -- extraordinary!
TONY BLAIR	There's a huge number of Americans -- [...]
QUEEN ELIZABETH	Well, exactly, yeah, they're all very much sort of spread around. And not only in London, you know, but all parts of the Country.
TONY BLAIR	I know the Americans are looking forward to the visit, anyway.
QUEEN ELIZABETH	But I-I -- don't find myself saying, you know, it's not new to us, 'cause we were there fifteen years ago.

(BBC *Monarchy: The Royal Family at Work*, 2007, ep.1, min. 26:20)

First of all, what is most striking at the eye of the readers of this excerpt is the fact the Queen's utterances are not as fluid as they might expect based on her public speeches. This difference is absolutely normal, and the difference between a Passage Reading Style and a Casual style has already been pointed out, with the latter being characterised by a scarce self-monitoring.

---

48 In a fly-on-the-wall documentary, the troupe works as unobtrusively as possible, usually by setting cameras in the rooms. The physical absence of the cameramen might help the protagonists forget about cameras and act more naturally.
49 The transcriptions in this chapter are mine, with the support of online softwares for audio transcription and the help of mother-tongue acquaintances.

However, the traditional representation of the upper-class speaker in the fictional dialogue (see Chapter 4) has arguably reinforced the idea that the members of the aristocracy speak more fluidly and with a more precise articulation of sounds. This passage, on the other hand, confirms Phillipps's words (1984, 37–38 – see also section 2.1.3) on the fact that fluidity should not be taken as a requirement for natural upper-class speech. The Queen's utterances contain several hesitations and reformulations, which are part of the phenomenon known as 'repair' (Sidnell 2016). Repair, or in this case 'self-repair,' starts when there is a disjunction with a preceding talk, a so-called 'trouble source,' which is overcome by solution or abandonment (ibid., quoting Schegloff et al. 1977 and Schegloff 2000). The same casualness is also sometimes reflected in the use of vague expressions (e.g. 'sort of,' which is abundantly used by the Queen), discourse fillers (e.g. 'you know') and contractions (e.g. ''cause' instead of 'because').

From the phonological point of view, some U-RP traditional features that can be distinctively heard in this passage are in bold in the text. These include, for example, the use of [ɔ] instead of /ɒ/ in 'lot' and the phenomenon of smoothing in the words 'yesterday' and 'years.' Wells (1998, 239) mentions other types of diphthongs (PRICE and MOUTH) where the sound is 'smoothed' and turned into a monophthong, but these two words are clearly pronounced by the Queen as, respectively, [jɜstəːdeː] and [jəːz]. Moreover, there is a wide use of tapped-R and [ɪ] in HAPPY words, although it is not consistent but limited to specific words; 'very' contains both features every time it is uttered, and so does the adjective 'extraordinary.' 'Country' also ends with an open vowel, which is also rather long in this case, thus [kʌntɹɪː], but there is a retroflex approximant rather than a tap, like in 'spread.' 'Only,' on the other hand, is pronounced [əʊnliː] and it is an example of Happy-tensing.

In the previous chapters it was often emphasised how suprasegmental phonology is one of the most defining aspects of aristocratic speech, and the Queen's intonation and voice quality are the elements that mark a clear distinction between her spoken language and that of Tony Blair in this passage. According to Thomas (2013, 119–120), the analysis of voice quality takes into consideration both laryngeal factors and supralaryngeal factors; as for the former, which involves the setting of the vocal folds, a certain 'creakiness' can be heard, but this might be due to a physiological ageing of the speaker, whose early recordings show an almost complete absence of roughness. A distinctive 'plumminess' (Wells 1992, 283 – see section 1.3.1), which occurs when the larynx is lowered and the oro-pharynx is widened, can be perceived throughout the whole documentary. As regards supralaryngeal factors, which have to do with settings above the larynx, the main aspect to be noted is the Queen's abundant use of rounded lips.

It is also interesting to point out the difference in terms of intonation between the Queen and Tony Blair. In particular, while the Prime Minister's tone can be defined as rather low, on the whole, the Queen's talk is extremely high-pitched, as the waveform below shows.[50]

Waveform 1 – The Queen and Tony Blair, prosodic comparison

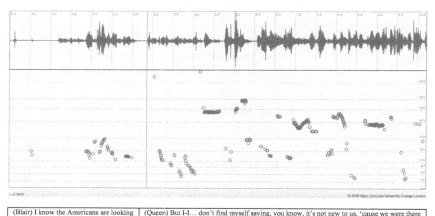

(Blair) I know the Americans are looking forward to the visit, anyway.	(Queen) But I-I... don't find myself saying, you know, it's not new to us, 'cause we were there fifteen years ago.

Tony Blair is often considered as a speaker of Estuary English (Watson-Smyth 1999, De Pascale 2013, 100, among others), but, as argued by Wells (1998, quoted in De Pascale 2013, 101), he exhibits a certain flexibility and a good command of situational accent shift. In his conversation with

---

50 This waveform, and also the following ones, were obtained through WASP (Waveform, Annotations, Spectrogram & Pitch), a software for the analysis of speech (see footnote 4).

the Queen there are neither glottalised stops nor vocalised laterals, and it can be safely argued that he speaks quite a pure form of RP, but prosody is what really differentiates his 'neutral' language from the upper-class tone of Queen Elizabeth.

In the next excerpt, taken from episode 4, *The Queen and Us*, the Queen is talking to one of her secretaries and a difference in tone is audible in this scene too. The waveform of a short part of this conversation follows the transcription below.

– Scene 2:

QUEEN ELIZABETH	I was actually rather amused by this -- it's a frightfully good idea.
SECRETARY	Yes, the hats.
QUEEN ELIZABETH	It's this usual thing -- why wasn't I wearing a crown, you see? And, well, you have to say -- well, it's too heavy to travel with. I think that's good fun too. Very inventive children, aren't they?
SECRETARY	It's quite astonishing. No-one could work out what the boy said, ma'am, outside the library when he took -- he was very keen on taking the flowers – uhm, I think just you came out of the library.
QUEEN ELIZABETH	No, no, he just -- 'cause I had a copy in my hand -- he hadn't got one, you see, so I think he thought it was for them. He just took it and went away. Sweet. Doesn't often happen.

(*BBC Monarchy: The Royal Family at Work*, 2007, ep.4, min. 23:05)

The prosody of the Queen's interlocutor is, in this case, more variable compared to that of Tony Blair. Her secretary's speech, in fact, reaches some high pitches, but it is not as constant as the Queen's talk, whose amplitude in terms of both pitches and edges is rather remarkable (see waveform below). From the point of view of voice quality, the Queen's does not lose her 'plumminess' and the use of rounded lips is in this case combined especially with the pronunciation of affricates. Such phenomenon is particularly marked when she utters the word 'children.' The pronunciation of the word 'frightfully' also contributes in adding an emphatic effect, and, in fact, it is taken by Wells (1992, 283) as an example of one of the most frequent circumstances in U-RP where "the steady-state of a consonant" (ibid.) is prolonged; as a consequence of this prolongation, the following unstressed vowel is elided, thus [fraɪt:flɪ] instead of /fraɪtfəlɪ/.

Waveform 2 – The Queen and secretary, prosodic comparison.

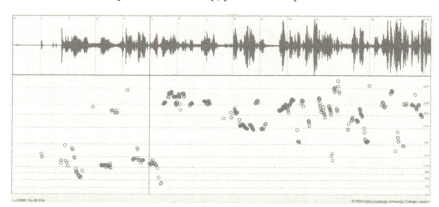

(Secretary) […] he was very keen on taking the flowers -- uhm, I think just you came out of the library.	(Queen) No, no, he just -- 'cause I had a copy in my hand -- he hadn't got one, you see, so I think he thought it was for them. He just took it and went away. Sweet. Doesn't often happen.

In this passage, too, there is no doubt that the style of the Queen is casual, with no self-control on language, which is made evident through the frequent hesitations, reformulations, fillers (e.g. 'you see') and contractions (e.g. ''cause,' again). This leads us to imply that the upper-class peculiar prosody is not a speech style to be acquired for purposes of social re-affirmation, but it is a real defining aspect of the language of the aristocratic people regardless of the context in which they find themselves.

As regards the phonological aspects of this scene, it has in common with the first one the phenomenon of 'smoothing' of the diphthong /eɪ/; thus, we have 'say' [se:] and 'away' [əwe:]. Moreover, both [ɾ] and [ɪ] can be heard again in the word 'very,' and the latter is also clearly audible in the word 'heavy.' Another quite marked feature is the emphasis on plosive sound /p/ in 'happen,' which causes a nasal release, peculiar of U-RP speech.

As far as the other features that are generally associated with U-RP (Wells 1992 – see table 4 in Chapter 1), such as the [ɪn] variant and the open TRAP vowel, there were no traces of them in the passages of *Monarchy: The*

Royal Family at Work that were examined, which arguably suggests an actual change in the Queen's language, now closer to mainstream RP. Such process, however, is still not complete, because features like tapped-R and the open HAPPY vowel are still sometimes adopted by Elizabeth II. The following diagrams show the frequency of these two phonological features compared to that of their 'mainstream' counter-parts in the passages that have been analysed.

Table 5 – HAPPY-tensing and rhoticity in *Monarchy: The Royal Family at Work*

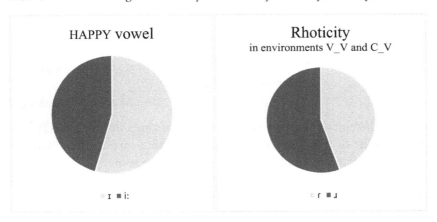

The second documentary that was selected to analyse the language of Queen Elizabeth is *The Coronation*, directed by Harvey Lilley in 2018 and narrated by Keeley Hawes. It is one-hour long and it was realised to mark the 65th anniversary of the Queen's coronation. It is presented by Alistair Bruce of Crionaich, Sky News commentator and 'coronation expert,' in form of a candid conversation. It was reported on *The Guardian* that "the tone was only ever momentarily reverential, and when it slipped into that squishy territory it was usually the Queen herself who yanked it back out on dry land" (Mangan 2018). Therefore, thanks to its 'casualness,' the recording is perfect material for natural language analysis, especially because before that occasion the Queen had always been reticent to engage in official interviews (Barry 2018).

In *The Coronation*, Bruce and the Queen talk about the royal crown, i.e. St. Edward's Crown, its history and its characteristics, and the Queen describes the experience of her coronation while watching some pictures and footages of the ceremony, which took place on 2nd June 1953 in Westminster Abbey. A personal transcription of all the salient parts of the film from the linguistic point of view, followed by their linguistic analysis, is provided below.

– Scene 3:

QUEEN ELIZABETH	But it's -- it's still as heavy? Yes, it is. It weighs a ton. It's very solid, isn't it?
ALISTAIR BRUCE	Ma'am, I don't suppose you've seen it much.
QUEEN ELIZABETH	No, I haven't. Thank Goodness!
	And it's impossible to tell which is front and back, I suppose. It's identical, I think.

(BBC The Coronation, 2018, 3:58)

From the beginning of the conversation with her interviewer, it is very clear that the tone of the Queen is on the whole rather casual. The absence of a self-monitoring and pre-planning of her speech is made evident, again, through the hesitations, but also through the exclamations (i.e., "Thank Goodness") and the frequent use of question tags (i.e., "isn't it?") and fillers (i.e., "I suppose" and "I think"). The informality of the conversation is also emphasised by the fact that these cues of natural speech are uttered with a lack of precise articulation of all their phonemes, thus we hear the omission of /ə/ in the first syllable of 'suppose' and of /t/ in "isn't it." This last phenomenon is particularly surprising, because upper-class speech, and RP in general, is usually described as an accent whose plosive consonants are always clearly pronounced. It has to be underlined, however, that this is more a process of T-dropping than glottaling or glottalisation, which are loaded with a social stigma, as it has often been pointed out in the previous chapters.

The traditional open HAPPY vowel is clearly audible in the word 'heavy,' and this also happens in scene 6 (see below), although the same word was pronounced with a HAPPY-tensing in the previous documentary (see scene 2). The phenomenon of centring of vowel sounds, peculiar of U-RP, is more intense in the following scene.

– Scene 4:

ALISTAIR BRUCE	It's always difficult to -- always remember that diamonds are stones. So, very heavy.
QUEEN ELIZABETH	Yes. Fortunately, my father and I have about the same sort of shape head. Once you put it on, it stays. I mean, it just remains itself.
ALISTAIR BRUCE	You have to keep you head raised still.
QUEEN ELIZABETH	Yes, and you can't look down to read the speech. You have to take the speech up. Because if you did, your neck would break. It would fall off. So, there are some disadvantages to crowns, but otherwise they're quite important things.

(BBC *The Coronation*, 2018, 8:10)

The diphthongisation of the TRAP vowel, signalled by Wells (1992, 281) as the first recognisable feature of U-RP, is not very frequent in the present-day spoken language of Queen Elizabeth, while the CLOTH lexical set is more frequently marked, although the scholar argues it is an old-fashioned feature (ibid., 282); in scene 4 in particular, 'off' is pronounced [ɔf] instead of /ɒf/. Sometimes, when /ɔ/ is already the RP standard phoneme, like in 'fortunately,' 'fall' and 'important,' the Queen tends to slightly raise the sound even further, between [ɵ] and [o]. The same as 'off' happens with the word 'lot' in scene 5 below.

– Scene 5:

| ALISTAIR BRUCE | What did the two children do for the rest of the day? Can you remember, ma'am? |
| QUEEN ELIZABETH | No, dear, I wasn't there. I wasn't there, I have no idea what they did. But there are a lot of other people in the palace as well, I think, lots of children. |

(BBC *The Coronation*, 2018, 25:10)

What is striking of scene 5 is the high level of informality and casualness, which can be read in the script through the use of the exclamation 'dear' and the repetition of "I wasn't there." The intonation, however, is extremely 'U,' with rather high pitches and edges and a noticeable rounded position of lips is noticeable during the utterance of /tʃ/ in 'children' (see also scene 2). The following waveform shows a big amplitude of the waves of the Queen's speech compared to Bruce's:

Waveform 3 – The Queen and Alistar Bruce, prosodic comparison

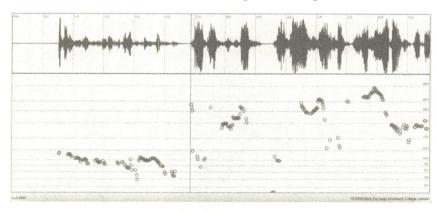

(Bruce) What did the two children do for the rest of the day? Can you remember, ma'am?	(Queen) No, dear, I wasn't there. I wasn't there. I have no idea what they did.

This waveform corresponds to scene 5 and it was taken just as an example of the prosodic difference between the two speakers, which is constant in most parts of the documentary. For example, scene 6 below also contains extremely high pitches, especially when the Queen uses sudden exclamations (e.g., "No!"):

– Scene 6:

ALISTAIR BRUCE	Heavy?
QUEEN ELIZABETH	Well, I think it's three pounds, or something. Quite heavy.
ALISTAIR BRUCE	Comfortable, ma'am?
QUEEN ELIZABETH	No! Nothing like that is comfortable. The more jewels, the better. George III invented that, didn't he?
ALISTAIR BRUCE	I think so, ma'am, yes.
QUEEN ELIZABETH	Mh. He loved jewellery and -- colour.

(*BBC The Coronation*, 2018, 40:14)

Apart from the high-pitched prosody, the aristocratic effect of the Queen's language is again conveyed through the use of [ɪ] in 'heavy' and also through the opening of the central vowel /ə/ in words like 'better' and 'colour,' which are pronounced as [bɜtɑː] and [kʌlɑː]. This is more or less the same phenomenon that, according to Wells (1992, 281), happens in U-RP with the centring diphthongs, although it is a monophthong in this case. As regards diphthongs, instead, in this scene the phenomenon of 'smoothing' can be traced in the sound /aʊ/ of the word 'pound,' thus rendered as [paːnd].

Not an actual 'smoothing,' but rather a tendency to turn diphthongs in monophthongs, can also be noted in scene 7 below:

– Scene 7:

QUEEN ELIZABETH   It's -- It's the sort, I suppose -- the sort of beginning of one's life, really, as -- as a sovereign. It's a sort of pageant of chivalry and old-fashioned way of doing things, really. But it's quite interesting to have it, you know.
I mean, I've seen one coronation and been the recipient of the other. It is pretty remarkable.

(*BBC The Coronation*, 2018, 43:33)

The old-fashioned pronunciation of the word 'really' as [ɹɪːlɪ], or even [ɹeːlɪ], rather than with the diphthong /ɪə/, is highly noticeable in the speech of many U-RP speakers of the older generation, and this is frequently recognised as a marker by filmmakers. This feature is widely used in *The Crown*, but also in *Downton Abbey* by the character of the Dowager Lady Violet. Nevertheless, at present there are no linguistic studies on this phenomenon, which is not even included in Wells's taxonomy on U-RP phonological facts (1992).

From this section on the language of Queen Elizabeth, it results that she is undoubtedly a U-RP speaker, although not all the U-RP traditional features are used consistently in every linguistic context. The TRAP and HAPPY vowels, but also tapped-R, for example, are still adopted, but only sporadically, while the use of [ɔː] in CLOTH and the 'smoothing' of diphthongs – considered by both Ross (1959) and Wells (1992) as secondary aspects at the time of their writing – has arguably increased. Thanks to the prosodic analysis of parts of the Queen's utterances in conversations, it was also possible to point out that the traditional aristocratic intonation and voice quality as described by Wells (1992) is maintained by Queen Elizabeth in the casual speech style, whereas a perfect phonological articulation and precision of language are not always observed; hesitations, reformulations and vague language ("I suppose" and "sort of," in particular, are widely repeated) are very frequent throughout the whole corpus that was examined.

3.2. The Royal Family

This section will provide a short outline on the spoken language of some of the other members of the Royal Family, with a focus on the younger generation. This language was defined by Wales (1994) as 'Royalese,' and it was later quoted by Goodman (1997) to refer to "a group of linguistic features widely associated in Britain with the speech of the members of the Royal Family, as well as certain other high status groups" (ibid., 197, also quoted in Di Martino 2012, 63–64).

Several reviewers consider the accent of Prince Philip to be very similar to that of his wife, and to some extent their son's idiolect is also not too different either (Lohr 1992 and Schmid 1999, quoted in De Pascale 2013, 115–116). Referring to the difference in accent between Prince Charles and his late wife Lady Diana Spencer, Lohr (1992) talks about a "Charles-Di split," which is "a matter of two styles of upper-class speech," as confirmed by Wales (1994, 5) too; Charles, in fact, despite adopting a slightly more modern U-RP than his parents (Schmid 1999), speaks with a rather conservative accent, whereas Diana had "swung to the other end of the RP spectrum, occasionally assuming a trendy down-market variant, including traces of popular London speech, that approaches Cockney." (Lohr 1992).

The case of Lady Diana is quite interesting because her native accent was U-RP, owing to her aristocratic background, but she later shifted towards a more 'relaxed' accent, contaminated by working-class features, such as T-glottaling (De Pascale 2013, 114–115). This was also pointed out by Rosewarne (1984, 3) in his article on Estuary English, where he wrote that "Princess Diana was once heard saying 'There's a lo(?) of i(?) abou(?)'" (ibid.).

Lady Diana was certainly the most innovative member of the Royal Family from the linguistic point of view, since the use of some non-standard variants contributed in turning her into the most beloved figure in modern British culture. Her two sons apparently developed the same kind of accent, a variety of RP with some regionalisms and contemporary features, as Smith (2011) puts it, which distinguishes them from their father and grandparents. In the case of Prince William, commentators define his accent as still being 'cut-glass' (see section 1.3.1), but they also argue that it is 'less polished' than that of his wife (Smith 2011; Copping 2012). In

De Pascale's opinion (2013, 123–125), William went even further than his mother, whom she identifies as an Advanced-RP speaker (see also Wales 1994, 5), following Gimson's definition (see Chapter 1), and suggested that he often adopts a full urban accent, with a frequent use of glottal stops and L-vocalisation both in informal-tone interviews and public speeches. Kate Middleton, instead, showed no use of these socially-marked features; on the contrary, her RP accent sounds much more refined and more similar to that of the older generation of the Royal Family, despite the fact that she has got upper-middle class origins and no real aristocratic ancestry (ibid., 125–128; Copping 2012). In her phonological analysis of William and Kate's interview that was aired on ITV News in November 2010, De Pascale (2013) emphasises the fact that the linguistic divide between the two fiancées is very clear.

> The observation of the excerpt gives evidence of the lack of L-vocalisation and T-glottalling in the speech of Miss Catherine Middleton compared with the same set of words uttered by Prince William. [...] The extracts also display a 'marked' pronunciation of the /t/ sound by Miss Middleton, as if she wanted to stress the accent distance between her and Prince William. Actually, she marked this sound even in those words and phonological contexts where T-glottalling is described as a prestige innovation in Received Pronunciation (ibid., 127).

Following De Pascale's words (ibid.), it might be assumed that, although the tone of the interview was generally casual and unplanned, Kate maintained a self-monitoring on her language, with the aim of conforming to the new status she was about to acquire. As it was discussed in the previous chapters, the obsession to conform to the prescriptive linguistic norms is a charac-teristic of the middle classes, whereas the members of the upper class do not feel the same social insecurity; in 2010, Kate Middleton was still a 'commoner,' therefore her social pressure to use the 'U' form of RP was understandable, but apparently the linguistic gap between William and her is still noticeable. This might be due to another factor, namely the social pressure that Kate may feel, probably unconsciously, as a woman. In fact, as it was discussed in section 2.2.1, women and men are still associated to different social roles and social behaviours, and women are generally expected to adhere more to the linguistic norms compared to their male peers, who are allowed to use informal and non-standard features without being misjudged (Trudgill 2000, 72–73).

Despite the advances in the policies related to gender equality, the gap between males and females is apparently still present today even among the youngest generations. As it was reported in *The Daily Express*, some phoneticians argued that Princess Charlotte picked up her mother's pronunciation, while Prince George and Prince Louis sound less 'posh' and use some features of Estuary English like their father (Ferguson 2020). Experts Geoff Lindsay and Jane Setter, in particular, expressed that this phonological distance is clearly noticeable from a recent video clip where the three children address some questions to BBC broadcaster and natural historian David Attenborough (ibid.). The transcription of the three questions is as follows:[51]

GEORGE   Hello, David Attenborough. What animal do you think will become
            extinct next?
            [...]
CHARLOTTE   Hello, David Attenborough. I like spiders, do you like spiders too?
            [...]
LOUIS   What animal do you like?
            [...]

Both doctor Lindsay and professor Setter argue that George and Louis's accents are clearly closer to Estuary English than Charlotte's pronunciation, basing on their use of L-vocalisation in the word 'animal' (with a final [ʊ] that replaces /l/) (ibid.); however, it must be noted that from these short extracts there is no trace of other features of Estuary English, and in Charlotte's utterance there is not a similar phonological context to verify if she pronounces /l/ according to RP or Estuary English, therefore an expanded acoustic analysis to confirm the thesis on her supposed 'higher' accent would be needed. From the prosodic point of view, their intonation is very similar, with medium-high pitches.

As regards Prince Harry, his idiolect is very similar to that of his brother, a variety of RP contaminated by urban features, which Smith (2011) defines as a form of Near RP, following Wells's terminology (1992). What is interesting to note is the supposed influence of his wife's American accent on his language, but some reviewers argue that the opposite is also sometimes noticeable (Gillet 2019; Liwag Dixon 2020).

---

51 Watch the video at https://www.youtube.com/results?search_query=royal+chil
   dren+attenborough (last accessed 10/11/2020).

3.3. Linguistic features of some British upper-class celebrities

The Royal Family can definitely be considered as the emblem of the British nobility and studying the language of this restricted speech community provides valuable data for the study of upper-class English in Britain. However, although several contacts and 'intrusions' have occurred, it is still a rather self-contained group of people who share a very similar background; it is, therefore, interesting to integrate the discussion on the royal members' spoken language with that of other popular personalities with an aristocratic descent but who are not directly connected to the Crown.

One of the most famous aristocratic families of the twentieth century is definitely the Mitford family and, in particular, the Mitford sisters, the six daughters of David Freeman-Mitford, Baron Redesdale, and his wife Sydney Bowles.[52] The eldest daughter, Nancy, as it was mentioned at the beginning of this thesis, was the protagonist of the 1950s 'U/non-U debate' (Ranzato 2018, 205) and disseminated Alan Ross's acronyms and definitions related to upper-class speech (1954 – see Chapter 1). She even asked him a revised version of his article that she later re-published in a volume with other insights about the upper classes by novelists and journalists, where she also included the article "The English Aristocracy," which she had previously published on the literary magazine *Encounter* (1955) (ibid.). This book, whose title is *Noblesse Oblige: An Enquiry into the Identifiable Characteristics of the English Aristocracy*, was published for the first time in 1956 and contains different perspectives of the debate, for example the vexed reaction of novelist Evelyn Waugh on the inanity of the whole matter. Nancy Mitford was also primarily a novelist, and some of her stories are a depiction of the British upper class in the early twentieth century, based mostly on her family. As it was showed in section 1.3.3, she used some of her characters to make some metalinguistic comments on upper-class language, and Professor Ross admitted he had taken inspiration from Mitford's *The Pursuit of Love* (1945) to compile his list of 'U' and 'non-U' words.

---

52 To know more about the Mitfords see the book by Lovell (2001) and the sisters' letters collected by Mosley (2007).

Nancy Mitford had a very clear view on how an aristocratic person should speak, so it is interesting to include a short passage of her speaking in this chapter on upper-class English in the natural dialogue:

NANCY MITFORD   [...] My father, who was a very clever person in his way, quite uneducated himself, like a peasant, like a very clever peasant, [...] he heard from somebody, I don't know who, that if girls went to school, they'd develop thick calves from playing hockey. And he was very much against these thick calves. He thought it was hideous -- and so, our education was completely neglected.

(BBC *Nancy Mitford: A Portrait by Her Sisters*, 1980, min. 16:58)

This extract is taken from a 1966 interview to Nancy Mitford, later included in the BBC documentary *Nancy Mitford: A Portrait by Her Sisters*, filmed by Julian Jebb in 1980, where her sisters Pamela, Jessica and Deborah discuss her life and works. This passage is very short, but, in a less-than-one-minute speech, Mitford adopted more than one feature listed by Wells (1992) in his description of Upper-crust RP, such as an extremely open HAPPY vowel ('somebody' is pronounced [sʌmbədɜ]) and a clear tapped-R ('very' [vɜɾɪ]). Also, like in the case of the Queen (see section 3.1), a monophthongisation of /eɪ/ into [e:] is quite noticeable in the word 'way' and 'playing,' where the [ɪn] variant is also present. As regards the prosodic aspect, Mitford's intonation contains extremely high pitches and edges, and her voice is often laryngealised, but her lips were rounded less frequently than the Queen's. In short, Nancy Mitford was the perfect example of the 'U' speech as it was described by Ross (1954, 1959) and by Wells (1992), but it must be underlined that in this case we are dealing with a recording dated 1966 and featuring a person who was fully aware of the importance of language as a social indicator.

The most recent recording of a member of the Mitford family is an interview to the youngest sister, Deborah, the Dowager Duchess of Devonshire. In this interview, which she gave in 2010 for PBS, she presents her book of memoirs *Wait for Me* (2010).[53]

---

53 Part of this interview can be viewed at the following link: https://www.youtube. com/watch?v=DSAbSRcsUcY (las accessed 20/11/2020).

DEBORAH MITFORD   The title -- the title was fairly obvious if you're the youngest of seven children -- and you're about two, and you've learnt to talk, sort of, and you can't keep up. It was always "Wait for me! Wait for me!" because my poor stubby legs couldn't go quick enough.

[...]

I first met Andrew in April 1938, when we were both just 18, and -- we met at a dinner party. A very ordinary way of meeting then, because -- the famous coming out, which had an utter different meaning -- and in those days you were not meant to dance twice with the same person.

[...]

The accent of the Duchess of Devonshire in this passage is very similar to that of the Queen, based on the analysis that was conducted in section 3.1. In particular, the open HAPPY vowel and tapped-R are not too marked, like in the case of her sister Nancy, but her speech sounds 'U' thanks to other features, especially the laryngealised voice, the use of rounded lips while uttering affricate sounds (e.g. in 'children') and the phenomenon of 'smoothing;' thus, we have, for instance, 'title' [taːtl], 'days' [deːs] and 'twice' [twaːs]. These few data from the analysis of the accent of Deborah Devonshire let us conclude that the results from previous studies on the 'democratisation' of the Queen's speech (Harrington et al. 2000; Harrington 2005; Richards 2018) can be confirmed and might also be extended to the older generation of the British upper class in general, at least based on the frequency of phenomena like Happy-tensing and the loss of rhoticity. Conversely, the traditional, peculiar intonation and voice quality are retained, together with an increase in the use of monophthongisation.

As far as the younger generation is concerned, apart from the members of the Royal Family, one of the popular upper-class people to whom the population can relate when thinking about the aristocracy today is certainly comedian Miranda Hart. Despite her aristocratic background, Hart declared she did not consider herself to be part of the upper class (Roche 2012), but we know from her TV and cinema roles that she speaks an aristocratic language. Among her most popular roles there is the character of Chummy in *Call the Midwife* (2012–present), an "emblematic U-RP speaker" (Ranzato 2018, 216), and she has recently played Miss Bates in the latest film adaptation of Jane Austen's *Emma* (de Wilde 2020). In terms of phonological rendition, her every-day casual language is probably closer to Mainstream RP than to U-RP, but from the prosodic point of view she sounds rather aristocratic. It is probably for her natural intonation that she is often cast in film and television productions where an upper-class character is needed, and this can be related to what Kozloff (2000, 61) defines as an 'opportunity for star turn'[54] (see next chapter).

3.4. Final discussion

The qualitative linguistic and acoustic analysis of the audiovisual corpus of this chapter, conducted under the principles of Sociophonetics and Conversation Analysis, was meant to provide innovative insights on present-day upper-class English in natural dialogue. In particular, by combining the data from the speech analysis of the Queen (both her past and present-day language) and that of other members of the Royal Family and the British aristocracy, it is possible to propose the following conclusions:

- such features as the open TRAP vowel and the [ɪn] variant, which were very frequent in U-RP until the first half of the twentieth century, are now almost disappearing;
- [i] in HAPPY words and tapped-R are still used sporadically, but they are confined to specific words, like for example in 'very;'
- the use of [ɔ] in the CLOTH lexical set and the phenomenon of 'smoothing' have arguably increased in frequency;
- 'U' prosody and voice quality are still unchanged and they are perhaps the most defining aspects of upper-class English today, whose phonological system has become much closer to the so-called Mainstream RP.

---

54 'Star turn' is also one of the categories in which instances of accented dialogue are classified in the website *Dialects in Audiovisual* (https://dialectsinav. wixsite.com/home/), a project coordinated by Irene Ranzato and to which I am a contributor.

Chapter 4 Upper-class English in audiovisuals: the case of *The Crown*

4.1. The language of upper-class characters in audiovisual dialogue

In the last few decades, the adoption of accents and dialects in cinema and television has been one of the most common techniques to build characters' identity through language. As noted by Hodson, the dialogue is often used by filmmakers as a 'shortcut' to portray characters' socio-cultural background, drawing on audiences' "impression that they know what a dialect sounds like and what characteristics a speaker of that dialect is likely to have [...]" (2014, 11). In short, consciously or not, they usually rely on the social meaning of on-screen 'clichéd dialects,' in Kozloff's words (2000, 82), to locate each character in more or less specific categories, even if such process leads to linguistic stereotyping (Lippi-Green 2012, 101–126; Hodson 2014, 60–79). Although it is necessary to remark a distinction between represented and real dialect, the former is still largely adopted as a tool to make films sound more 'realistic' (ibid., 206–2015).

Realism is generally the ultimate aim for the use of accented voices in films and TV series, not only to portray individual characters, but also to characterise a whole social group. Social class differentiation has been, in fact, conveyed through language especially starting from the 1960s with the British 'new wave' cinema, which concentrated mostly on the depiction of the lower classes (Hallam and Marshment 2000, 24; Wagg 1998, 11; Hodson 2014, 206). The British upper classes, on the other hand, have been traditionally characterised by the use of RP in cinema and TV productions, but some attempts at representing the upper-class sociolect can also be mentioned, especially in the last few decades. As argued by Ranzato (2018, 205), most of the times the stereotyped and old-fashioned representations of this class mirror the 'U/non-U debate' that was mentioned in the previous chapters, but there are also recent examples of a realistic linguistic depiction of upper-class members, and not only as in contrast with working-class characters. One could also argue that the upper-class character has become a meme, i.e., "a unit of cultural transmission" (Hayes 2020, 94) that is associated to a specific kind of language variety, which Hayes (ibid.), drawing on Dawkins's theory (1976), put forward by Chesterman (1997), calls 'dialectal meme:'

> While accents themselves could fall within the parameters of a meme, I see them as a token or a fragment of a much larger sign that is a sociolinguistic meme of identity, which I will call a 'dialectal meme': dialect referring to the linguistic qualities of dialect and accent; and meme referring to the surrounding ideas of identity attached to that dialect and/or accent. From this point of view, accent could be the Peircean sign, and the meme the object. As for an interpretant, when an accent or dialect is perceived in an utterance, this triggers its meme to be engaged in our psyche, unleashing a labyrinth of 'memetic signs,' on diatopic, diastratic, idiosyncratic and diachronic levels. These four facets of memetic signs will henceforth be considered as housed in and carried by the dialectal meme (ibid., 94–95).

This chapter will be devoted to the discussion of the linguistic rendition of the upper-class figure in the audiovisual dialogue, and this first section will include an outline of the most significative cases in British cinema and television, together with a discussion of the main functions that this sociolect generally performs in the telecinematic dialogue. This section will serve as an overview to show the incidence of U-RP to characterise upper-class characters, and it will hopefully be useful for the reader as a guide to look for filmic instances of this accent. A qualitative linguistic analysis of the idiolects of the main characters of *The Crown* will then follow in a separate section, and it will be conducted according to the principles of Sociophonetics and Conversation Analysis. *The Crown* was chosen as a case study because almost all the characters in the series are members of the upper class and their social status is realistically reflected in their language, thus providing for several phonological, prosodic, but also lexical elements to discuss. Finally, the chapter will end with a short insight on the rendition of the upper-class talk in audiovisual translation.

*

If we consider U-RP as a full language variety, similar in its basic phonological structure to Mainstream RP but culturally separate from it, we will find that there are not so many instances of this accent in nowadays cinema and television. Some of the characters speaking an almost authentic upper-class British English were classified by Ranzato (2018, 212–223) into different *topoi*, which will be briefly summarised:

o *'All-upstairs' dramas:*
The term 'all-upstairs' has been proposed by Ranzato (ibid., 212) to refer to those audiovisual productions that are set in an aristocratic context and whose protagonists have only a limited interaction with characters from different socio-cultural backgrounds. These productions generally portray the royalty, and the use of U-RP is generally aimed at conveying a socio-historical realistic effect through language. Films like *The Queen* (2006) and *The King's Speech* (2010) are to be included in this group, as well as TV series such as *The Crown* (see section 4.2 for a wider discussion and analysis). The functions of the use of upper-class speech in these contexts are generally two: first of all, the temporal and spatial collocation of the story through language, and, secondly, it is used to portray real people, as it is the case of the three titles that have just been mentioned.

o *The Adoptive U-RP:*
In *Educating Rita* (1983), we find an instance of metalinguistic reflection when the protagonist, the Liverpudlian hairdresser Rita, switches to U-RP to sound more educated. In Ranzato's opinion (ibid., 213), this is a case of transformative style-shifting, which occurs when a speaker shifts to another variety because he/she considers it to be 'better' than his/her native language. At a certain point in the film, Rita mimics the aristocratic accent of her roommate to build a new identity of herself, and she does that by using a refined lexicon and syntax combined with the typical prosody of U-RP. This form of 'adoptive U-RP,' whose label was proposed by Ranzato (ibid.), building on Wells's notion of Adoptive RP (1992, 283 – see also Chapter 1), is also to be found in the use of U-RP by Mancunian Ella in *East is East* (1999) to sound more courteous in front of some distinguished guests (ibid., 2014), but also more recently in the TV series *Glee* (2009–2015), where we hear, in a couple of occasions, the character of Becky thinking in U-RP.

o *Upper class vs. working class:*
This category includes all of those cinema and TV productions where the depiction of the upper classes is juxtaposed to that of the lower classes, and the resources of the language are often exploited to emphasise social differentiations between characters. A case in point is *Downton Abbey* (2010–2015), but also *Gosford Park* (2001) and *Upstairs Downstairs* (both the 1971 film and the series aired on TV between 2010 and 2012 – Ranzato 2018, 215), where the use of U-RP is generally aimed at providing a social commentary. Sandrelli (2016) wrote an article about language variation in *Downton Abbey* and how it was rendered in the Italian dubbed version, and Bruti and Vignozzi (2016) dealt with the sociolinguistic landscape in *Gosford Park*; both studies will be discussed in section 4.3, explicitly dedicated to upper-class English and AVT.
Ranzato has also discussed in other contexts the social differentiation of characters in James Ivory's filmic adaptation (1985) of the novel *A Room with a View* (1908) by E.M. Forster, observing that Daniel Day-Lewis affected a 'snobbish' language in his interpretation of Cecil, especially through his tone and voice quality, which is in contrast with Julian Sand's George Emerson (2016, 10). In Ivory's film, there are also other actors who have a long tradition of portrayals of upper-class characters, namely Helena Bonham Carter and Maggie Smith. The former, who is an authentic RP speaker, adopted a more conservative accent in another Ivory's adaptation from Forster, *Howards End* (1992), where she plays the part of Helen Schlegel, whose 'posh' language is in contrast with that of Leonard Bast (Hodson 2014, 136–143).
The upper-class language variety, however, stands out even more in those cases in which an aristocratic character is included in a working-class environment; it was already mentioned in section 3.3, in fact, that the character played by Miranda Hart in *Call the Midwife* (2012–present), Chummy, can be considered as an emblematic U-RP speaker, and her linguistic contrast with the rest of the characters is clearly audible. In particular, she makes an abundant use of intensifying adverbs and a refined and old-fashioned lexicon with an upper-class 'plummy' tone (Ranzato 2017, 37–39; 2018, 215). When one isolated character speaks with an aristocratic voice, its function in the fictional dialogue is not only that of showing a social differentiation between characters, but it can also serve

to provide the character with a recognisable idiolect, especially if the actor/actress is particularly talented in rendering a convincing upper-class language, thus taking advantage of his/her opportunity for a star turn.

o *British as upper class vs. American as working class:*
The opposition between British characters portrayed as upper-class people with a refined attitude and Americans as easy-going working-class people has quite a long tradition in English-language cinema. The British upper-class characters generally speak Mainstream RP in these films, but occasionally we find cases in which U-RP is adopted to underline even more this stereotypical social distance. *A Fish Called Wanda* (1988), for instance, features an upper-middle-class family, whose U-RP accent is humorously in contrast with that of a group of American thieves, and the purpose if this linguistic distance is to emphasise the stereotype of the wealthy, educated, but also cold and snob British, against the poor and passionate American (ibid., 220–221).

It is not rare for the prototype of the British aristocrat to be shown as living with butlers and housekeepers, and people with the highest servant status are generally extended the use of RP or U-RP, especially when they have an interaction with American characters, as it happens in episode 4x24 of *Friends*, as Ranzato observes (ibid.),[55] when one of the main characters, Phoebe, has a dialogue with a British housekeeper, but also in films like *The Grass is Greener* (1960) and *The Remains of the Day* (1993 – ibid.), and TV series *The Fresh Prince of Bel-Air* (1990–1996 – Zabalbeascoa 2021, 196-199).

o *The British Villain:*
British English, and particularly RP, often characterises the evil character in many American productions, perhaps building on the idea that the RP speaker is usually part of a social élite that appears rather distant to the ordinary American viewer (Ranzato 2018, 223). In other words, the use of the British variety is a way to build a cultural 'otherness' (Zabalbeascoa 2021, building on Di Giovanni 2003, but see also Iaia 2018). Zabalbeascoa (ibid.) and Lippi-Green (2012, 122) mention as an

---

55 See also Ranzato 2021 for an extended discussion on the *topos* of the butler in audiovisuals.

emblematic example the case of Jeremy Irons's filmography, both as an actor and as a dubber for animated films.

The use of U-RP instead of Mainstream RP to characterise an evil or unpleasant character occurs when there are other British actors in the cast, like in the case of Veruca (Julia Winter) and Mr Salt (James Fox, arguably a case of 'star turn' as an upper-class character) in *Charlie and the Chocolate Factory*, or when the entire production is British and a 'heightened' and 'posher' accent than RP is needed. A case in point is the villainous character of Bellatrix in the *Harry Potter* saga (2001–2011), played by Helena Bonham Carter, who, as it was previously mentioned, is deeply familiar with the upper-class speech.

Audio instances of all the films and TV series that were mentioned in this section can be viewed in the *Dialects in Audiovisuals* website (Ranzato et al. 2017),[56] which is a repository of files on English-language audiovisual products whose leading or recurring characters use a regional variety of British English. Although some of the files also include sporadic insights and specifications on the use of social varieties, the main aim of the project is that of categorising films and TV series according to diatopic variation, which is why there is no specific section on U-RP and all the products featuring this social variety are included in the "Received Pronunciation" section.

Regarding the functions of this accent in the audiovisual dialogue, the main tendency that emerges from a general consultation of the website is that of using it to provide a social commentary.[57] U-RP is a social-class accent, therefore it is not a surprise that it is mainly employed to characterise the members of the upper strata of society, especially when they have a prolonged interaction with characters from the lower classes. Another frequent function is that of 'British vs. American,' which puts forth a tendency to portray British characters in an American context as aristocrats, and, vice versa, American characters who go in the UK often end up being in an

---

56 Read the rationale of the project at the following link: https://dialectsinav. wixsite.com/home/rationale (last accessed 10/03/2021).

57 The observations coming from the consultation of *Dialects in Audiovisuals* are personal conclusions that have not been confirmed by a systematic quantitative study yet.

upper-class context. These two functions are occasionally combined with that of eliciting humour, especially in comedies that rely on stereotypical social and regional differences, but also with that of locating the time and place of the story. Following the taxonomy of the *Dialects in Audiovisuals* website, this last function was quoted as a unit, yet in the case of U-RP it might be intended more as a marker of 'time,' namely as an old-fashioned accent that serves to describe characters from the old generations. The 'villain' function appears only rarely, owing to the fact that its real label on the website is 'British villain,' meaning that it is usually found in American productions, and for the American audience Mainstream RP is 'distant' enough to characterise an upper-class evil character. As it was previously suggested, U-RP for villains is more functional in British productions, but in these cases other language varieties are also traditionally adopted for villainous people, like Cockney, for example (Ranzato 2019). Finally, upper-class language is often adopted in the audiovisual dialogue to provide a realistic portrayal of real people, especially in the case of period dramas, and this is the main function of U-RP accent in *The Crown* (see next section).

On a purely linguistic level, it has to be clarified that not all the traditional phonological features of U-RP are used in all the films and TV series that are identified as containing instances of it, but what they all share is the distinctive upper-class tone and voice quality, which include the lowering of the larynx and opening of the oropharynx, peculiarly high pitches of tone and the occasional use of rounded lips. From the syntactical and lexical point of view, complex and obsolete forms are generally preferred by upper-class characters. These aspects will be analysed and discussed in the next section, which is dedicated specifically to the case study of *The Crown*.

4.2. *The Crown*

The Crown is an historical drama series that explores the most salient private and public events of the British Royal Family from the end of George VI's reign and throughout the long reign of Queen Elizabeth II. It was created and written by Peter Morgan: the first season was broadcast on Netflix in 2016, and the second one in 2017. After a total change of cast, a third season was broadcast in 2019 and a fourth one in 2020. The series received a critical and audience acclaim and was also awarded several accolades, such as the Golden Globe for Best Television Drama Series in 2017 and in 2021. In 2019, *The Guardian* included it in the list of the best 100 TV series of twenty-first century.

As some reviewers have highlighted, historical events are not always accurate and real history is used as a mere starting point to make drama (see, among others, Samuelson 2016 and Noonan 2017). The fourth season, in particular, was highly criticised by some commentators, who argued that the series "ranged from historical inaccuracy [...] to a propensity to flesh out the narrative with half-truths and downright falsities" (Bastin 2020). Author Simon Jenkins even defined it as a "cowardly abuse of artistic license" (2020), and British Minister Oliver Dowden suggested that the series should include a disclaimer at the beginning that clearly states that what is shown in the episodes is "a beautifully-produced work of fiction." (Arkin 2020). Netflix, however, has announced that there is no need for a fiction warning, because the audience will know it is just drama (Bastin 2020). There is also a part of critics that argues that the fictionalisation of the events in the life of the royal members should not be seen as a troubling matter, since inaccuracy is not a synonym of untruthfulness. An interesting anonymous insight in *The Economist* (2020), in particular, has recently pointed out that, all in all, the Windsors are not badly portrayed in the series, but they are simply shown as having struggles related to their inner conflict between duty and personal fulfilment (ibid.); in the same article, it can be read that "if the monarchy is so vulnerable that a man pretending to be Prince Charles saying mean things to a woman pretending to be his wife damages it gravely, then the institution has probably outlived its usefulness. Famous people are often portrayed in ways they do not like, but that is one of the costs of free speech." (ibid.). Despite this debate, a few scholars, such as Bondebjerg (2020) and Pearson (2021), argued that *The Crown* is undoubtedly a quality product, and that its great popularity is mainly due to the fact that it is about the British monarchy, arguably one of the brands that are easier to sell nowadays. Peter Morgan had proof of the appeal of the royal brand with his previous projects, the feature film *The Queen* (2006) and the theatrical drama *The Audience* (2013), and Netflix had been proved that a period drama like *Downton Abbey* could attract a remarkable number of American viewers, therefore they were both convinced that a product like *The Crown* could be internationally successful and was thus worthy of a big investment (Pearson 2021). US audience data also demonstrated that Morgan's series played a fundamental role in enticing the older generation to access the streaming service (ibid.).

From the narrative point of view, Abbiss (2020) points out that *The Crown* adopts a post-heritage approach[58] to its central theme of the role of the monarchy in modern society; the historical gaze of the show links the past to the present through the depiction of recurring traumatic events that do not find any resolution (ibid., 92). In addition to this, the series shows an influence from the twenty-first-century Nordic Noir drama,[59] particularly from the aesthetic point of view, through the adoption of frequent moments of stillness and reflection and a psychological connection between places and characters (ibid., 93). According to the scholar, the approach of *The Crown* appears less deferential than other dramas concerning the British monarchy, and this is how he describes the negotiation of history and fiction in this serial drama:

> The central conflict between Elizabeth's public and private identities connects the serial's concept to its negotiation of fact and fiction, allowing *The Crown* to acknowledge its acts of speculation through recurring motifs of the media and the use of archival material.[...] In *The Crown*, inclusion contributes to the serial's ambiguity, acknowledging that multiple interpretations of its central characters and the monarchy as a whole are possible. The historical gazes of Elizabeth, Philip and Margaret further display what is concealed and revealed by *The Crown*'s narrative, encouraging the media-literate viewer to negotiate the drama's ambiguities and recognise that it does not offer a definitive interpretation of the royal family (ibid., 109).

Leaving aside the narrative conflict between historical and fictional, from the point of view of language representation it can be argued that *The Crown* is characterised by an evident realism. Ranzato (2017, 36–37 and 2018, 212–213), in particular, commented on the accent adopted by actress Claire Foy, who played the role of the Queen during the first two seasons, arguing that she simulated a convincing U-RP, both in her voice quality,

---

58 'Post-heritage' is a term coined by Claire Monk to identify the general approach of period dramas of the 1990s, which showed "a deep self-consciousness about how the past is represented" (2001, 7, quoted in Abbiss 2020, 7).
59 Nordic Noir is a subgenre of TV crime fiction, characterised by naturalistic settings, gloomy colours, frequent long takes and haunting music.

through the use of the so-called 'plumminess,' and in her phonological rendition. The scholar (ibid.), referring to Claire Foy's lines in episode 1x09, observed that she perfectly reproduced the open HAPPY vowel, the open second element in the NEAR diphthong, and the [ɪn] variant.

Foy herself and also some of her fellow-actors declared they worked intensely in order to achieve the accent, thanks to the presence of dialect coach William Conacher (Laneri 2017), and they mentioned that they were asked to pay special attention to the reproduction of vowel sounds. This is what Foy and Smith (Prince Philip in seasons 1 and 2) said about their language training:[60]

CLAIRE FOY   There's only one thing to know about that accent and it's that you need to say '*one*' [wʌn].
How do you say 'was,' Matt?
MATT SMITH   Oh, don't get me started on '*was* [wɒz]' and '*was* [wɔz].' I mean, for God's sake.
[…] Well, '*was* [wɔz]' was apparently the right way.

While Vanessa Kirby (Princess Margaret in seasons 1 and 2), in the same interview, declared:[61]

VANESSA KIRBY   It was such a weird accent to do and we ended up having to treat it like a dialect, because if you didn't, you ended up doing a sort of parody of posh accent […].
INTERVIEWER   Could you give me a line?
VANESSA KIRBY   *(in U-RP accent)* What would like me to *say* [seː]? It becomes very *easy* [izɪ], *because* [bɪkɔz] you have to practice so much.
[…] Yeah, it's things like *because* [bɪkɔz], and, I don't know, *actually* [ɜktʃuəlɪ].

From Kirby's use of U-RP during the interview, it might be assumed that the dialect coach of *The Crown* put special emphasis on teaching the cast how to reproduce the mid vowels in HAPPY and CLOTH, but also the phenomenon of 'smoothing,' which are, in fact, among the U-RP features that are still frequently used by upper-class people, as it was concluded at the end of the previous chapter. Speaking of the 'smoothing,' in particular, Foy later declared in an interview at *The Late Late Show with James Corden* that they were systematically reminded to pronounce the word 'house'

60 https://www.youtube.com/watch?v=S1MV9j0dPAQ, min. 1:40.
61 https://www.youtube.com/watch?v=S1MV9j0dPAQ, min. 3:00.

as [hɑːs].[62] From the point of view of voice quality, on the other hand, Conacher taught Foy not to open her mouth too much, to relax her jaw and to allow only a limited space between her teeth, thereby acquiring the peculiar 'plumminess' of the upper-class language (Laneri 2017).

What the actors and the dialect coach[63] said in interviews about the work on the accent is very interesting, because it confirms that an attentive linguistic research was included in the "quest for socio-historical realism" (Ranzato 2018, 212) that contributed in making the TV series a successful one. The linguistic realism of the product is one of the main reasons why it was chosen as a case study in this research; also, since this research seeks data that define a complete description of the upper-class sociolect and how this is represented in the fictional audiovisual dialogue, a product that showed mainly upper-class characters was needed, and *The Crown* is among the most recent 'all-upstairs' drama. The aristocratic English language is, in fact, the primary linguistic representation in the series, seeing that it follows the events of the Royal Family, which can be considered, as it was previously mentioned (see Chapter 3) as an example of a speech community. The upper-class sociolect is exclusively used to provide a realistic rendition of the entire social group and its function is neither that of contrasting characters with different social backgrounds, nor that of creating an aesthetic effect or a stereotypical reference to a specific identity. The unique function of the socially-marked language in *The Crown* is that of providing a portrait of real people, who either lived in the recent past or are still alive. Such aspect was fundamental in the process of choosing a case study for this chapter, considering that, in order to compare a dialect or an accent with its represented version, the latter requires a certain level of authenticity, and *The Crown* proved to be an example of that even from a first anecdotal evidence. Nevertheless, it must also be clarified that when we speak

---

62 https://www.youtube.com/watch?v=VBQWZmqb33I&list=LLmZWw7wwjwa oyzJ_IFIZDMA&index=25&t=0s, min. 0:20.

63 To know more about William Conacher's approach in training actors and actresses to reproduce accents, see Care (no date, https://www.spotlight.com/ news-and-advice/interviews-podcasts/perfecting-accent-work-with-dialect-coach-william-conacher/, last accessed 26/05/2021) and *Bow Street Academy* (2020, https://www.youtube.com/watch?v=3B6QKjm34IU&t=439s, last accessed 26/05/2021).

of linguistic authenticity in the audiovisual dialogue we must be aware of the fact that it is impossible to reach a full realistic representation of natural language. As many scholars in the field have pointed out (Kozloff 2000 and Richardson 2010, among other), a complete verisimilitude is not achievable and film/TV dialogue can only imitate spontaneous everyday speech because of issues of comprehensibility and conveyance of meaning at all levels (Richardson 2010, 45–47), which means that it is a type of text that is "written to be spoken as if not written" (Baños Piñero and Chaume 2009, quoting Gregory and Carroll 1978, 42); in other words, it is a 'prefabricated orality' (ibid.) that has to be understood by any hearer, which is why any aspects that might potentially compromise a full comprehensibility only find a limited and 'planned' space. At any rate, what can be safely affirmed is that *The Crown* reaches a fairly high level of verisimilitude from any point of view, and social, cultural and historical realism is achieved thanks also to the linguistic representation. The following sub-sections will be dedicated to this linguistic representation through the analysis of some parts of dialogues featuring different primary and secondary characters; the first two seasons are grouped separately from the last two, seeing that between seasons 2 and 3 the cast was completely renewed.

4.2.1. Seasons 1 and 2

The social group represented in *The Crown* is rather homogeneous from the socio-cultural point of view, yet there is a natural variety in terms of age and sex. In the dedicated file on the *Dialects in Audiovisual* website,[64] it is pointed out that the female cast in season 1 is characterised by a more conservative language compared to the idiolect of the main male characters, coherently to what generally happens in everyday life (see section 2.2.1) and what was also observed about the Royal Family (see section 3.2). Following the same general observation in Sociolinguistics, we would have expected to find a similar slight linguistic difference between the characters of the older generation and those of the younger generation, but, at least in season 1, there is no substantial variability according to the age of the

---

64 See the file at the following link: https://dialectsinav.wixsite.com/home/the-crown (last accessed 1/12/2020).

protagonists. All the female characters invariably speak a pure version of upper-class language and accent as described by Ross (1954 and 1959) and Wells (1992). The instance transcribed in the file on the website well shows this linguistic accuracy, which is why it will be partly quoted here and briefly discussed:

– Scene 1:

QUEEN ELIZABETH	How are you?
QUEEN MARY	I am always happy to see you, and my mood will improve yet further if you promise me one thing.
QUEEN ELIZABETH	Name it.
QUEEN MARY	Not to ask me how I am, it's all anyone ever does. Forget death by lung disease, it's death by bad conversation.
QUEEN ELIZABETH	Alright, I promise. But if you are feeling up to it, there was something I wanted to talk to you about.
QUEEN MARY	Fire away.
QUEEN ELIZABETH	I was listening to the **wireless** this morning, where they described this fog as an act of God.

(*The Crown*, 1x04, min. 19:12)

In this scene, there is no linguistic distance between the young Queen Elizabeth and her grandmother. On the contrary, it might be argued that some of the traditional features of U-RP are here even more emphasised by Elizabeth, while Queen Mary's (Eileen Atkins) RP accent is perhaps more natural and fluent. In fact, her accent sounds 'posh' mainly because she speaks with a semi-closed mouth and rounded lips, causing the traditional upper-class 'plumminess,' whereas Foy affected a U-RP accent by working not only on voice quality but also on the adoption of a general raised vowel system, especially in the TRAP and CLOTH lexical set (i.e., 'act' is pronounced as [ɜkt] and 'God' as [gɔd]). Also, she pronounces the word 'you' in her first line more as [jə] than /juː/, accordingly to what Conacher taught her to do: "The queen doesn't say, 'Thank you'; the queen says, 'Thenk you,' with the 'you' very short," says Conacher. "I can tell you that was one of the most addictive things to say on the set... We would all, the entire crew, go around saying, 'Thenk yu.'" (Laneri 2017).

Furthermore, from the lexical point of view, it is interesting to note Queen Elizabeth's use of the word 'wireless' to indicate the radio; such choice is coherent to the prescription provided by Alan Ross (1959), who described the language of the upper-classes more or less in the same period in which Scene 1 is set (1953). In particular, the scholar wrote that 'radio' is the non-U form of 'wireless,' but it is the U word for a type of aircraft (ibid., 19).

Arguably, an attentive study of the upper-class accent and language in the 1950s and 1960s preceded the writing of the dialogues in seasons 1 and 2, and perhaps age variability was not taken into consideration because it was a minor aspect compared to the linguistic difference between the younger and the older generation today (see section 3.2). Young Queen Elizabeth's speech, in fact, is not more innovative than that of her mother either, as it can be observed by reading Scene 2 below.

– Scene 2:

QUEEN MOTHER	Well, call me if you need anything.
	[...]
	You won't, of course. You don't need me anymore at all.
QUEEN ELIZABETH	Yes, of course I do.
QUEEN MARY	No, you don't. Neither of you does. I have two grown-up daughters **quite** capable of looking after themselves now.
QUEEN ELIZABETH	Who is it -- you are stay**ing** with?
QUEEN MARY	The Vyners. Up in Caithness at the Northern Gate. Dunnet Head.
QUEEN ELIZABETH	Goodness. That's the end of the world.
QUEEN MARY	Yes. A chance to really get away from it all. To have a good think.
QUEEN ELIZABETH	About what?
QUEEN MARY	Everything.
QUEEN ELIZABETH	Well, don't think too much. Or too deeply. It just gets **one** in a muddle.
QUEEN MARY	Oh, by the way, I've arranged for Margaret to deputise for me while I'm gone, as a Head of State.
QUEEN ELIZABETH	Why?
QUEEN MARY	Well, someone needs to do it. Can't have people turning up for knighthoods and some civil servants heading them out.

(*The Crown*, 1x08, min. 10:50)

In this scene, too, there is no evident linguistic distance between the two characters, despite the fact that they belong to two different generations. On the contrary, it is, once again, young Elizabeth who adopts more frequently the main features of U-RP: her final '-y' is generally pronounced as [ɪ] (e.g., 'deeply,' in scene 2), she makes a consistent use of the old-fashioned [ɪn] variant (e.g., 'staying' [steɪn]) and she often 'smooths' her diphthongs (e.g., 'why' [waː]). The Queen Mother (played by Victoria Hamilton in seasons 1 and 2), on the other hand, does not seem to emphasise these features much, but she makes quite a wide use of the 'ʊ' open-mid vowel in CLOTH words (e.g., 'all' and 'gone' in this scene). However, generally speaking, it cannot be said that the accent of Queen Elizabeth sounds 'posher' than that of her mother in the series, because they both speak with an emphatic upper-class prosody. What stands out of Hamilton's representation of the Queen Mother's speech, in particular, is the extremely rising and high-pitched intonation, which is similar to that used for questions, as the following waveform shows.

Waveform 4 – The Queen and The Queen Mother (*The Crown*, 1x08, 10:57)

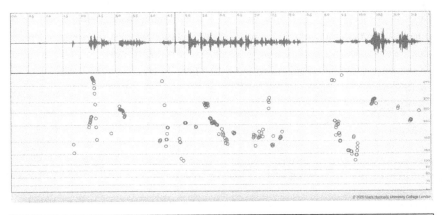

(Queen Mother) No, you don't. Neither of you does. I have two grown-up daughters quite capaple of looking after themselves now.	(Queen) Who is it -- you are staying with?

On the top of the waveform, it can be noticed that the amplitude of the speech of the two characters in the selected part of Scene 2 is rather limited compared, for example, to the waveforms shown in Chapter 3. This is due to the fact that the volume of their utterances is quite low, being a private conversation in a room with an open door; yet, although their tones are low, their lines produce extremely high pitches and edges, especially the Queen Mother's, which are not questions, in this case, but simple statements.

Also, apart from their prosody, both characters share a refined language from the syntactical and lexical point of view. For example, as it was mentioned in section 2.1.3, 'quite' has been used for a long time by the upper classes with an intensifying meaning rather than to moderate (Phillipps 1994, 78), and this appears to be the sense the Queen Mother attaches to the use of this adverb in Scene 2. Another 'U' feature in Scene 2 is the substitution of the perhaps more natural 'you' with the impersonal 'one' in Queen Elizabeth's utterance "It just gets one in a muddle" (Wales 1994, Goodman 1997, Fox 2004, 204, but see also section 1.3.2).

From the phonological point of view, the character who uses U-RP features the most, apart from Queen Elizabeth, is undoubtedly Princess Margaret (Vanessa Kirby). This might be due to the fact that, after the Queen and Prince Philip, she is the character with the highest number of lines in the first two seasons, therefore the dialect coach must have spent a long time training her. After all, Kirby herself declared she used to speak the accent together with Claire Foy even when not filming so as to practise the upper-class talk (see link in footnote 62). The next scene which will be examined is the representation of a private conversation between the two characters.

– Scene 3:

PRINCESS MARGARET	I brought a copy of the statement which we'll give to the newspapers tomorrow.
	[...]
QUEEN ELIZABETH	We're going to have to delay it.
PRINCESS MARGARET	Delay what?
QUEEN ELIZABETH	The announcement. [...] Because of the baby.
PRINCESS MARGARET	What baby?
QUEEN ELIZABETH	Mine. I'm expecting.

(*The Crown*, 2x07, min. 28:12)

All in all, Margaret's accent sounds as 'U' as that of Elizabeth, except perhaps for a less accentuated 'plumminess.' If we just read the script, the style does not look particularly elevated, but it is actually a rather neutral conversation between two people that know each other. Acoustically speaking, however, this dialogue sounds very 'posh' to the average hearer, owing to the presence of several instances of U-RP. For example, the open HAPPY vowel is clearly audible, like in Margaret's way of pronouncing the word 'copy' [cɔpɪ] (where we also find [ɔ] instead of /ɒ/) and especially in 'baby' [beɪbɛ], whose last vowel is remarkably open, even more than Elizabeth's pronunciation in the previous line (i.e., [beɪbɪ]). Moreover, she also makes use of the nasal release after the plosive consonant in 'statement' and she turns final dental plosives into affricates (e.g., 'what' [wɔtʃ]) as much as her sister does, like in 'it' and in 'announcement' in this scene, but also in all the similar contexts in Scenes 1 and 2 previously discussed. Such feature is not mentioned in any of the studies on the language of the upper classes that have been quoted in this volume, and the analysis of the natural upper-class English in Chapter 3 did not provide as a result a relevant frequency of this feature;[65] nevertheless, it is widely used in *The Crown*, especially by the younger actors and actresses, and this might be due to a couple of reasons. First of all, this might be a suggestion of Conacher, the official dialect coach of the series, who has perhaps noticed this phonological tendency in the speech of the members of the Royal Family; secondly, the affricate sound may be the consequence of an 'over articulation' of people who generally do not clearly articulate final plosives and who end up realising a sort of lenition of /t/[66] (see Buizza and Plug 2012 for a discussion on the phenomena related to /t/ in modern RP). This theory also rises from the anecdotal evidence that the accent of the same characters in seasons 3 and 4, played by Olivia Colman (Queen Elizabeth) and Helena Bonham Carter (Princess Margaret), who are natural RP speakers, does not include this phenomenon frequently, apart from sporadic occurrences in surprised expressions (e.g., "What?"). Colman and Bonham Carter proved to be perfect U-RP speakers (see next section), and they probably sound more natural than Foy

---

65 It ought to be taken into account, however, that the analysis in Chapter 3 was conducted mostly on recordings of the last three decades, while the first two seasons of *The Crown* are set in the 1950s and 1960s.

66 Such an argument is not supported by a solid research, it is a simple intuition, which would be interesting to convert into the initial research question for a future study.

and Kirby, not only because RP is their every-day accent, but also because they are more experienced in playing royal roles.[67]

A slight difference in accent, on the other hand, can be heard in the private conversations between the Queen and her husband. The accent of Prince Philip (Matt Smith in seasons 1 and 2) is arguably closer to a Mainstream RP, since he rarely uses mid vowels in HAPPY or TRAP, although he does more consistently in CLOTH, and he never 'smooths' his diphthongs. One instance of a private conversation between the Queen and her husband is included in section 4.3, while here another similar comparison between the monarch and a male voice will be provided:

– Scene 4:

PORCHEY	Hello?
QUEEN ELIZABETH	Porchey. I hope I'm not **disturbing**.
PORCHEY	**Goodness.**

(*The Crown*, 1x09, min. 8:19)

In Scene 4, Queen Elizabeth is speaking at the telephone with her old friend Porchey (Joseph Kloska), with whom she shares her passion for horses. 'Porchey' is a nickname that comes from the courtesy title of Lord Porchester, by which Henry Herbert was known from his birth until 1987, when he succeeded his father as the 7th Earl of Carnarvon. Therefore, he was undoubtedly a member of the British nobility and he had more or less the same age as the Queen; he was not part of the Royal Family like the characters that have been mentioned until now, but he had close contacts with Buckingham Palace and his socio-cultural background was very similar to that of Elizabeth. In the series, however, Porchey's accent sounds slightly less refined than that of the Queen, who, for example, uses the old-fashioned [ɪn] variant in "disturbing" in this scene, while her friend can be defined more as Mainstream RP speaker from the phonological point view. His voice quality, on the contrary, has got all the characteristics of upper-class prosody, and some of his lexical choices define his class belonging too. The expression "goodness" to show surprise, for example, despite not being

---

of exclusive use of upper-class people, is arguably used quite often by the English élite (see also Scene 2), as the anecdotal evidence from the small corpus of documentaries and interviews used for the analysis of Chapter 3 showed. Another 'U' word, according to the discussion in Chapter 1, is 'papa' to refer to one's father (see section 1.3.3), which Porchey uses in Scene 5 below, where he is talking about King George's favourite horse.

– Scene 5:

PORCHEY	I remember getting the phone call from your father, when he was born. By Hyperion and out of Angelola.
QUEEN ELIZABETH	Yes. We gave him his first milk. Do you remember?
PORCHEY	Watching him grow up, everyone thought his elder brother would be the star, but your clever papa always had an instinct for this one.

(*The Crown*, 1x09, min. 8:19)

Apart from using the French 'papa' as an alternative to 'father,' Porchey uses the typical upper-class intonation with several high pitches, but his articulation of words is noticeably less precise than Elizabeth's pronunciation. The speed with which he utters the first line, in particular, leads him to produce a 'weak' /t/ sound in "getting" and "out," which is more similar to a flap rather than a plosive consonant.

Other characters in the series that are members of the British upper class, but not of the Royal Family, are Mr and Mrs Churchill. In fact, Winston Churchill (played by John Lithgow) was a descendant of the Duke of Marlborough, and his wife Clementine (played by Harriet Walter) was the granddaughter of the 10th Earl of Airlie. From the linguistic point of view, the comparison of their accent in the series follows the same pattern that was previously mentioned regarding the couples Elizabeth-Philip and Elizabeth-Porchey, with the female component using a higher frequency of U-RP features, as the analysis of Scene 6 below will point out.

– Scene 6:

| CLEMENTINE | Are you winning? |
| WINSTON | Uh, no. There was one brief tantalising moment when I thought I had it. I moved in for kill. But then one wrong brushstroke and it got away once again. |

CLEMENTINE   I've just been talking to Jock about your 80ᵗʰ birthday.
WINSTON   Oh, no, don't mention it.
CLEMENTINE   Because it happens on the same day as the opening of the Parliament, they've decided to combine events and hold a reception in your honour at the Great Hall.

(*The Crown*, 1x09, min. 6:04)

Clementine's lines in Scene 6 contain several phenomena that are considered as typical of the upper classes, as it was observed throughout the whole book; some instances are the use of the alveolar [n] instead of the velar /ŋ/ in "winning" and "talking" and the reduction of the diphthong /eɪ/ into [eː] in words like "day" and "same." Also, she pronounces "because" with a back open-mid vowel, [bɪkɔz], which was considered as marker of upper-class speech by the dialect coach of the series (see link in footnote 62). Churchill's vowels, on the contrary, are more similar to Mainstream RP (except, perhaps, for a remarkably open and long sound in "had," [hæːd]), although his voice quality and his sophisticated language undoubtedly prove him an aristocrat (see section 5.2 in the following chapter for further discussion on Churchill's language).

4.2.2. Seasons 3 and 4

A slight linguistic distance between Queen Elizabeth and Prince Philip can be perceived in seasons 3 and 4, too, but it is perhaps less evident than in the previous two seasons. The role of Philip in the last two seasons is interpreted by Tobias Menzies, who affected a more marked 'U' prosody than Matt Smith by maintaining his mouth very closed while speaking, thus achieving the typical upper-class 'plummy' voice that was mentioned several times. In any case, the fact that, in both cases, Philip's accent contains less U-RP features than Elizabeth's must not be necessarily interpreted as a lack of training by the actors, but it might be due to a conscious decision of the creator and the dialect coach; not only is he a man, and therefore stereotypically allowed a more 'relaxed' language, but he is also an 'acquired' member of the British Royal Family, and this might have been taken into consideration. This is particularly evident through the use of a more 'mainstream' vowel system, as it was confirmed by the analysis of Scene 7 below.

- Scene 7:

PRINCE PHILIP	The trip was supposed to be a week. You were gone almost a month.
QUEEN ELIZABETH	Yes.
PRINCE PHILIP	With Porchey?
QUEEN ELIZABETH	Yes. [...] We went on racing business. It was a fact-finding expedition. [...] If you have something to say, say it now.

(The Crown, 3x05, min. 52:28)

Philip pronounces HAPPY words with the modern /iː/ and CLOTH words with a regular /ɒ/, and this last feature is especially evident in the different ways in which Menzies and Colman pronounce "was" in Scene 7: while the former says [wɒz], as any other RP speaker nowadays, the latter says [wɔz], which is the 'U' variant, as it was mentioned in section 4.3. Also, Colman is always very careful in replacing the diphthong /eɪ/ with the single long vowel [eː] (e.g., "say" in Scene 7), and her lines contain informal expressions only very rarely, while Prince Philip uses slang more frequently in private conversations, as shown in Scene 8, where he is reporting some rumours about Prime Minister Edward Heath to his wife.

- Scene 8:

PRINCE PHILIP	Apparently, there was a doctor's daughter. It was love at first sight. And she waited for him throughout the war, only for Heath to **chicken out** at the last moment. So, she married someone else.
QUEEN ELIZABETH	Where did you get all this from?
PRINCE PHILIP	Some **chap** I met, who knew Heath of old. Thinks that he, uh - - never moved past it. [...] There you are. When you find the right one, **snap 'em up**.

(The Crown, 3x09, min. 11:24)

In Scene 8, Philip uses two very informal expressions, 'to chicken out' and 'to snap up,' and he also starts a sentence by omitting the subject (i.e., "Thinks that he [...]"), which confirms the idea that men are allowed a more informal and less refined language than their female peers in high society too (see Chapter 2). The fact that he pronounces these expressions with his usual 'U' tone and his use of the word 'chap' (typical of upper-class slang – see section 1.3.3), however, define him unmistakably as an upper-class member.

The same balance between informal and 'U' lexical choices is found in the speech of Prince Charles, played by Josh O'Connor. U-RP features are more frequent in his lines than in those of his father, but he is less consistent than his mother, and he is certainly one of the characters with the most peculiar prosody. O'Connor, in fact, declared he tried to render an accurate accent from the point of view of voice quality by clenching his teeth together most of the time, and added that the tip he used to reproduce this voice was by pronouncing the word 'yes' more or less like the word 'ears,'[68] very similarly to the way Colman pronounces the same word in Scene 7. An instance of this phenomenon is heard in Scene 9, in which we also find one of the informal expressions used by Philip in the previous extract.

– Scene 9:

PRINCE CHARLES	There is someone I **quite** like.
LORD MOUNTBATTEN	The one cheering you on today, yes?
PRINCE CHARLES	Yes. Who used to be with Andrew Parker-Bowles until they had a **falling out**. Over Anne. **If you please.**
LORD MOUNTBATTEN	Your sister?
PRINCE CHARLES	Don't ask. It's all **a bit messy**. But **the long and short of it** is Camilla is now free, and I'd like to **snap her up.**

(The Crown, 3x08, min. 15:50)

In Scene 9, Charles uses the expression 'to snap up,' like his father in Scene 8, thus suggesting that this informal phrasal verb is not uncommon among upper-class people. It is evident that the context is rather informal, because he also uses expressions like 'to have a falling out,' 'to be a bit messy' and other more courteous idioms, although not too formal, such as 'the long and short of it' and the exclamation 'if you please.' This kind of language well defines him as a young man who has a close relationship with his interlocutor and who is certainly an aristocrat, as highlighted by a few elements, such as his prosody and the 'U' usage of 'quite' to indicate

---

68 Watch the interview by Netflix UK & Ireland at https://www.youtube.com/watch?v=6zG0rMZQ55c&t=85s from minute 2:18 to 3:30 (last accessed 5/12/2020).

a big rather than a modest quantity (see section 2.1.3). Lord Mountbatten (Charles Dance in seasons 3 and 4) was Prince Philip's uncle and a distant cousin of the Queen, and he is represented in the series as having a similar accent to the other male characters, that is quite modern and 'mainstream' from a phonological perspective, but unmistakably 'U' from a prosodic one.

In season 4 we make the acquaintance of young Diana Spencer (Emma Corrin), whose language is rather 'posh' like the rest of the cast; after all, as it was pointed out in Chapter 3, she started to use features of Estuary English later in her life, so we might expect to find an evolution in her language in the next season. In Scene 10, a dialogue with Camilla Shand, played by Emerald Fennell, is shown.

– Scene 10:

CAMILLA The Prince of Wales told me he was going away for six weeks and not
         taking you. [...]
         I said "That's not very nice. Your poor brand-spanking-new, gorgeous,
         young fiancée, all alone in the house."
DIANA   Actually, left all alone in the palace.
         [...] Well, not the house.
CAMILLA That's what the Prince of Wales calls Buckingham Palace. It's what they
         all call it. "The house."

(*The Crown*, 4x03, min. 28:40)

In Scene 10, Diana is treated like an outsider of the Royal Family by Camilla, who refers to Buckingham Palace with the word 'house' as if she was a regular guest and Diana was inferior to her for not knowing the habits of the royals. Both women, however, were upper-class members and they could be considered as peers, because Diana was the 8th Earl Spencer's daughter and Camilla was the 3rd Baron Ashcomb's daughter. Their social status is perfectly reflected in their accent in the series, especially in prosodic terms, although in different ways. In fact, while Camilla's voice is perceived as 'U' mainly thanks to a remarkable amplitude of tone and frequent high pitches, Diana adopts a much lower and balanced tone and she manages to lower her larynx, thus achieving the typical upper-class voice quality, by uttering her lines with a constant semi-closed mouth. Emma Corrin explicitly declared this was her trick to mimic the typical royal voice (see the interview at the link in footnote 65), and it is not only perceived acoustically, but it is also a visible physical behaviour that she shares with her colleagues O'Connor and Menzies.[69]

From a phonological perspective, in the series Diana and Camilla generally use U-RP typical features more frequently than the male characters, but less frequently than the women of the older generation such as Queen Elizabeth and Princess Margaret. One instance in Scene 10 is the pronunciation of the word 'house' with a monophthong, [haːz], which is one of the phenomena that the cast was reminded to pay attention on, as it was previously mentioned (see Foy's interview at the link in footnote 63) and the pronunciation of 'Wales' as [weːlz]. Also, the TRAP vowel in "palace" is [ɛ] rather than the 'mainstream' /æ/.

Scene 11 below, where Camilla keeps bragging about knowing more details about Charles's habits than his new fiancée, contains a few other elements that are interesting to point out.

– Scene 11:

CAMILLA   He has a soft-boiled egg with everything. You must know that.
           And he never eats garlic. Because of this **bizarre** new rule, come
           suppertime, he's always **ravenous**.
DIANA   Which new rule?
CAMILLA   The lunch rule. [...] The Prince of Wales doesn't eat lunch. [...]
           [...]
DIANA   **Golly.** He obviously tells you everything.

(*The Crown*, 4x03, min. 30:42)

The dialogue in Scene 11 is characterised by the same elements that were previously mentioned, like the 'smoothing' of /eɪ/ and a perfect 'U' prosody, which is emphasised by Camilla's use of rounded lips combined with the final affricate sound in 'lunch.' The extract is also interesting for what concerns lexical choices, which define the communicative exchange both from the diaphasic and the diastratic point of view. In particular, some of the expressions and words used by Diana and Camilla are clearly informal, but they are not as common in middle-class and working-class social contexts

---

69 O'Connor's and Corrin's interpretations were particularly praised by the critics, and they both received a Golden Globe in 2021, respectively for Best Actor and Best Actress in a Television Series Drama.

as they are among people in the high society. 'Golly,' for instance, is an exclamation that is generally used exclusively by upper-class people (see section 1.3.3), as 'suppertime' is perhaps perceived as a rather old-fashioned and 'posh' word.[70] Arguably, people from the working classes would hardly use words such as 'bizarre' and 'ravenous' either.

As far as upper-class lexical choices are concerned, there is another dialogue in season 4 that appears to be rather interesting to quote. The scene features Princess Margaret (Helena Bonham Carter) correcting the language of Prime Minister Margaret Thatcher (Gillian Anderson),[71] who was not a member of the upper classes, thus providing for a metalinguistic comment on social class and linguistic etiquette.

– Scene 12:

PRINCESS MARGARET	Aren't you supposed to be out there stalking?
MARGARET THATCHER	Yes, I was, but your sister --
PRINCESS MARGARET	No, you don't call her that. You call her "the Queen." She's the Queen, not my sister. And that chair. No one sits in that chair.
MARGARET THATCHER	Oh, I beg your pardon.
PRINCESS MARGARET	God, don't say that either. Say "What." Begging for everything is desperate. Begging for pardon is common.

(*The Crown*, 4x02, min. 23:13)

After reprimanding Thatcher for referring to Queen Elizabeth as "her sister" rather than as a monarch, Princess Margaret also remarks that she should not use the expression "I beg your pardon" to apologise because it does not

---

70 As it was mentioned in section 1.3.3, 'supper' is defined by Fox (2004, 219) as an alternative to 'dinner' when it is a light informal/family meal. The author mentioned this only in relation to the fact that the word 'tea' to refer to the evening meal is not used in upper-class contexts, whereas 'supper' is acceptable, but she did not specify that it is of exclusive upper-class use. However, although no linguistic studies seem to have discussed this, some comments by British native speakers seem to confirm the idea that 'supper' is perceived as a 'posh' word in working-class contexts. Read, for example, the following article by *The Guardian* (2013): https://www.theguardian.com/lifeandstyle/2012/aug/03/tea-with-grayson-perry-supper-dinner (accessed 27/02/2021).

71 Thanks to her interpretation of Margaret Thatcher, Gillian Anderson won a Golden Globe for Best Supporting Actress in 2021.

suit her status. This expression, says the Princess, is for 'commoners,' and the word 'pardon' is, in fact, at the top of the 'Seven Deadly Sins' that the upper-class members consider as a social-class shibboleth, as argued by Fox (2004, 211) and as it was discussed in section 1.3.3. 'Pardon' is generally used by the lower classes when they wish to sound courteous and classy, but it apparently defines the exact opposite. In Scene 4, Thatcher uses the expression to apologise, in which case, we read in Ross (1959, 18), the 'U' correspondence would be "Sorry!", but Princess Margaret tells her she should have said "What?". In any case, the function of this dialogue is that of underlining the social distance between the Royal Family and Margaret Thatcher, who is shown as an outsider for her entire stay at Balmoral during the episode, and this metalinguistic moment was only one of her numerous *gaffes* as a non-aristocratic guest.

4.3. AVT strategies

If we consider the Italian adaptation of the films and TV series that have been mentioned in section 4.1, we will notice that the upper-class sociolect is rendered almost invariably with a Standard Italian accent. Omission is, in fact, the most common technique to tackle the problem of the transposition of dialectal varieties in general, as it resulted from numerous articles in the audiovisual translation field (Di Giovanni *et al.* 1994; Pavesi 1994; Ranzato 2006; Chiaro 2008, apart from those focusing on specific case studies), some of which are included in collective volumes (Federici 2009 and Armstrong and Federici 2016, among others) or academic journals (see, for example, the dedicated special issues of *inTRAlinea* – Marrano *et al.* 2009; Nadiani and Rundle 2012; Brenner and Helin 2016; Geyer and Dore 2020) on the topic. The general outcome of this extensive scholarly literature is that language varieties are usually loaded with cultural connotations which are deeply rooted in the source culture and which are very difficult to reproduce in the target text without creating undesired stereotypical effects. However, the case of the diastratic varieties seems to be easier to deal with, compared to diatopic ones, and the representation of the language of the upper classes has recently attracted the attention of some AVT scholars, who studied the English-Italian language pair.

Both Bruti and Vignozzi's (2016) and Sandrelli's (2016) analysis – the former on the translation of *Gosford Park* and the latter on *Downton Abbey* (2010–2015) – pointed out that, while the adoption of 'homogenizing conventions' (Sternberg 1981, quoted in Munday 2009, 181) proves to be the trend in the rendition of the upper-class speech, the adapters attempted at creating an elevated effect through the strategy of compensation, "which involves making up for the loss of a source text effect by recreating a similar effect in the target text through means that are specific to the target language and/or text" (Harvey 2001, 37). In particular, Bruti and Vignozzi argued that aristocratic characters in *Gosford Park* are given a distinctive quality through tone and timber (2016, 69), whereas Sandrelli noticed that the adapters of *Downton Abbey* used sparse archaic words and French loans to make the dialogues sound 'posh' (2016, 169–170). Thus, in both cases we find examples of the so-called "compensation in kind,"[72] which consists in using a different linguistic device from that of the source text to convey a similar effect (Hervey and Higgins 1992, 34); more specifically, phonological aspects of the upper-class speech were replaced by prosodic or lexical features in the Italian dubbed versions. Compensation strategies were adopted in both audiovisual products because they served as a tool of social differentiation between upper-class and working-class characters (whose language usually sounds more spontaneous and informal), while it will be interesting to verify whether the same expedients were adopted to characterise the language of the homogeneous aristocratic community in *The Crown*. Before showing an example and providing a discussion of the strategies, here is a comment by Ranzato (2018, 212) on the matter:

> There is not much to note about the Italian translation of the series in which all characters have been invariably and predictably rendered with a standard pronunciation. It can just be remarked, however, that unlike other audiovisual productions in which dubbing voices are carefully typecast, the Italian Elizabeth has a firmness and confidence of tone which is strikingly different from the overall unassertiveness and apparent fragility of the young Elizabeth. It can thus be concluded that the Italian version fails in one of the few points which could

---

72 In the case of *Downton Abbey*, we could also refer to a form of "compensation in place," since archaisms in the Italian translation do not always correspond to the same line in the source text (Sandrelli 2016, 187).

be controlled in the adaptation phase, that of voice quality. Lexical choices are also not always happy and, again, fail to compensate prosodic losses [...] (ibid.).

Building on this comment, a brief analysis of the Italian dubbed version and of the Italian subtitles of one scene will be provided. The scene was selected among the episodes of the second season, where actors, and especially Claire Foy, seem to emphasise their aristocratic accent more than in the first season, probably due to a greater confidence with it. More importantly, the following scene was selected because it depicts a private conversation between same-generation interlocutors with a close relationship, who are supposed to reproduce natural language usage in such a context. Dialogues, both the original and the Italian dubbed and subtitled versions, were transcribed from the original Netflix episodes.[73]

In spite of the fact that the lines above are taken from a private face-to-face conversation between Queen Elizabeth (Clair Foy) and her husband, Prince Philip (Matt Smith), they use a high and sophisticated register. Phonologically speaking, on the other hand, Elizabeth's accent sounds more 'U' than that of Philip (see previous section). In fact, accordingly to what was previously observed, Foy's almost-perfect reproduction of the aristocratic prosody and voice quality is supported by the use of an open HAPPY vowel in the word 'tidy' [taɪdɪ], but also in 'very' [vɛɾɪ], where a slight tapped /r/ can be heard as well. Moreover, she also makes abundant use of the affrication of dental plosives in final position, like in 'What's wrong with it? [ɪtʃ]' and 'à la mode [mɔdʒ],' and she tends to use rounded lips in words ending with the suffix '-tion.'

As regards the Italian dubbed version, the most notable aspect is the loss of upper-class features in Elizabeth's accent, which are slightly compensated by a rather high-pitched intonation, which sounds quite haughty compared to Philip's 'calm' tone. While this clashes with the way the creator built the character, as remarked by Ranzato (ibid.), it may be inferred that it was due to a conscious consideration, whose purpose was arguably that of providing the Italian Elizabeth's speech with an aristocratic flavour that could not be conveyed through the phonological device. Rendering any accent in

73 See Valleriani 2021b (forthcoming) for a deeper discussion on the Italian adaptation of *The Crown*.

Table 6 – Translation analysis of *The Crown*, 2x05, min. 15:00

	Original	Italian dubbing	Italian subtitles
Prince Philip	Why on earth would you do something like that to your hair?	Perché ti sei conciata la testa in quel modo?	Perché / ti sei conciata la testa in quel modo?
Queen Elizabeth	What's wrong with it? I thought it was tidy and… sensible. […] Apparently, it's very *à la mode.* All the regimental wives are wearing their hair like this now.	Non ti piace?È un'acconciatura ordinata… di buon gusto. […] A quanto pare è molto *à la mode.* Tutte le mogli dei reali hanno capelli così ora.	Che cos'hanno? / Pensavo che fossero ordinati / e… appropriati. […] A quanto pare è molto *à la mode.* / Tutte le mogli **reggimentali** / acconciano i capelli così.
Prince Philip	[…] It's certainly very practical. And should you ever feel compelled to ride a motorcycle, it could always double as a helmet. […] Sure it will provide ample protection against any falling masonry.	Be', sono sicuramente pratici. Se dovesse **venirti voglia** di guidare una motocicletta, potrebbero servirti da casco. […] Sono certo che ti **proteggerebbero** se dovesse caderti una tegola in testa.	Sicuramente è **molto pratico.** / E **qualora** ti venisse voglia / di andare in motocicletta, / potrebbero sempre **fungere** da casco. […] Sicuramente **fornirà ampia protezione** / contro la caduta di calcinacci.

the Italian dubbing is a highly demanding task, but in this particular case it would be almost impossible, simply because in Italian there are no realistic specific phonological features that are associated with the upper-class speech.[74] The dubbing team may have had this in mind when they let the

---

74 It might be argued that we do have some features that define the upper-class accent in Italian, such as the pronunciation of intervocalic 'r' with the sound [ʋ], as it was mentioned in footnote 16 in Chapter 1, but it is my opinion that such features are rather stereotypical and nowadays they are mainly used to affect the aristocratic speech in comedies and parodies. It is true that this stereotypical

Italian dubber use an extremely clear articulation of words which sounds at times almost declamatory even when she is chatting.

From the viewpoint of word choices, it can be noticed in Table 9 that the dubbing team did not make a great effort in building a high register: verbs like *venire voglia* ('to fancy') and *proteggere* ('to protect') are not formal enough compared to, respectively, 'feel compelled' and 'provide ample protection.' Lip sync concerns might have been the reasons for these choices specifically, although, as Ranzato expresses, the dubbing team of *The Crown* has not always considered it as a central issue (ibid., 213).

The Italian subtitles, on the contrary, show a more complex structure and more formal lexical choices, such as the old-fashioned *qualora* ('in case'), *fungere* ('to serve as') and *fornire* ('to provide'). The choice to translate 'masonry' with *calcinacci*, instead, perhaps sounds slightly informal compared to the more literal *muratura*, but subtitles show a general greater degree of formality compared to the dubbed version, and this is probably due to the fact that the translation is highly literal. The adherence to the ST is one of the features that differentiates the subtitling process from dubbing, but it must also be taken into consideration that literal translations are faster to carry out, and speed is the most important aspect that companies like Netflix demand of their adapters. Even though translating literally sometimes helps in creating a style similar to the original, it might also lead to awkward results, such as the use of *reggimentale*, which in Italian is more related to the military than the royal semantic area, and the use of the singular for the omitted subject *capelli* in "Sicuramente è molto pratico" and "fornirà ampia protezione," as a calque on the English uncountable noun 'hair.'

The outcomes from this short insight could be the starting point of a more extensive and quantitative corpus-based investigation on the entire show, and another interesting further step in this research could be the linguistic comparison between the first two seasons and the work of the

---

variant is grounded on real evidence, but I believe that if the characters in *The Crown* used sound [ʋ] in the Italian dubbed version, it would sound unrealistic and grotesque. However, this is only a personal impression based on anecdotal evidence, and a systematic linguistic study on the language of the Italian upper classes would certainly shed more light on this.

adapters of the third and fourth seasons, which were filmed with a complete change of cast.[75]

4.4. Final discussion

This chapter dealt with the use of upper-class English, more specifically of U-RP accent, in cinema and television. The first section, in particular, was aimed at delineating an outline of the main telecinematic contexts in which we generally find people speaking this accent and the function that this tends to acquire in the dialogue. By examining the files of the films and TV series containing instances of U-RP collected in the *Dialects in Audiovisuals* website, it was possible to observe that the main aim for the adoption of U-RP is usually that of providing a social commentary; however, some examples of the use of a 'posh' accent for other functions (e.g., conveying humour, building a stereotyped British character, offering the portrayal of real figures) were also mentioned. This section was useful to remark the fact that U-RP has become, especially in the last few decades, a tool to construct a certain kind of telecinematic persona.

The rest of the chapter was dedicated to the linguistic analysis of the Netflix TV series *The Crown*, an 'all-upstairs' drama (Ranzato 2018), whose use of the upper-class accent is almost exclusively that of depicting realistically the speech community of the Royal Family. The outcomes of the analysis are the following:

- the female characters generally speak a 'posher' accent than the male characters, who also tend to use colloquial expressions more often;
- the dialogues present no relevant variability according to the age of the characters, at least in the first two seasons;
- the most common features of U-RP in the text are the use of [ɔ] in the CLOTH lexical set and the traditional 'plummy' voice, as it was also observed in the analysis of natural upper-class language (Chapter 3);
- the mid vowels in HAPPY and TRAP, whose use is apparently in decline in the natural dialogue, is much more frequent in its audiovisual rendition;

---

75 The Italian dubbing company for the first two seasons of the show was Studio Asci and the dubbing director was Federico Zanandrea, while BTI Studios and Elda Olivieri worked on the third and fourth season.

- a frequent affrication of final dental plosives is clearly audible in the U-RP speech of some characters, although there appears no mention of it in scholarly literature dealing with this accent, nor similar data resulted from the analysis of natural upper-class English.

Finally, the chapter ended with a short discussion on the strategies adopted to render the 'U' talk in Italian dubbing and subtitles; apparently, although the most common strategy is that of translating it with a neutral standard Italian, and *The Crown* was no exception, a few attempts at compensating through an extremely assertive voice quality in the dubbed version and sparse formal lexical choices in the subtitles was noticed.

Chapter 5   The Queen's speech: reality and fiction

5.1. Analysis of the Queen's speeches

The previous chapters offered a comparison between upper-class English in natural (Chapter 3) and audiovisual dialogue (Chapter 4) through the analysis of conversational spoken language, with the aim of providing innovative evidence on the spontaneous speech of British aristocrats. This last chapter will delve even further into the comparative aspect of the research by examining some real historical public speeches and how they were rendered fictionally in *The Crown*.

Public speeches are written texts made to be read orally, therefore they can be considered as forms of Passage Reading Style (Labov 1966/2006, 431, quoted in Hernández-Campoy 2016, 78). This style reaches an even higher level of formality than the Formal Style in speaking, because in this case the attention of the speaker is directed almost exclusively on his/her language, forasmuch as the content is pre-determined and the formulation of the message is not spontaneous (ibid.). In Labov (2006, 60–61), this style was designed to study the pronunciation of pre-determined diagnostic forms camouflaged in a text to be read by informants; public speeches, on the contrary, are not constructed with this explicit aim, but the analysis of this speech modality will offer further insights in terms of diaphasic variation of upper-class English.

Two famous speeches by Queen Elizabeth II will be analysed in this section. The first one is the first televised Royal Christmas message (1957), which was represented at the end of the fifth episode of the second season of *The Crown*. In this episode, the Queen decides to televise the upcoming Christmas message after a conversation with Lord Altrincham, who had written an article arguing that Royal public speeches were too oratorical and that the monarchy needed to adapt to the modern post-war society in general. In the following complete transcription[76] of this speech, the parts

---

76 The script of this speech was taken from the official website of the Royal Family (https://www.royal.uk/christmas-broadcast-1957, last accessed 15/12/2020).

in bold correspond to those represented in the TV series. A comparative phonological and prosodic analysis of the two versions will be provided.

- Speech 1:

Happy Christmas.

Twenty-five years ago my grandfather broadcast the first of these Christmas messages. Today is another landmark because television has made it possible for many of you to see me in your homes on Christmas Day. My own family often gather round to watch television as they are this moment, and that is how I imagine you now.

I very much hope that this new medium will make my Christmas message more personal and direct.

It is inevitable that I should seem a rather remote figure to many of you. A successor to the Kings and Queens of history; someone whose face may be familiar in newspapers and films but who never really touches your personal lives. But now at least for a few minutes I welcome you to the peace of my own home.

That it is possible for some of you to see me today is just another example of the speed at which things are changing all around us. Because of these changes I am not surprised that many people feel lost and unable to decide what to hold on to and what to discard. How to take advantage of the new life without losing the best of the old.

But it is not the new inventions which are the difficulty. The trouble is caused by unthinking people who carelessly throw away ageless ideals as if they were old and outworn machinery.

They would have religion thrown aside, morality in personal and public life made meaningless, honesty counted as foolishness and self-interest set up in place of self-restraint.

At this critical moment in our history we will certainly lose the trust and respect of the world if we just abandon those fundamental principles which guided the men and women who built the greatness of this country and Commonwealth.

Today we need a special kind of courage, not the kind needed in battle but a kind which makes us stand up for everything that we know is right, everything that is true and honest. We need the kind of courage that can withstand the subtle corruption of the cynics so that we can show the world that we are not afraid of the future.

It has always been easy to hate and destroy. To build and to cherish is much more difficult. That is why we can take a pride in the new Commonwealth we are building.

This year Ghana and Malaya joined our brotherhood. Both these countries are now entirely self-governing. Both achieved their new status amicably and peacefully.

This advance is a wonderful tribute to the efforts of men of goodwill who have worked together as friends, and I welcome these two countries with all my heart.

Last October I opened the new Canadian Parliament, and as you know this was the first time that any Sovereign had done so in Ottawa. Once again I was overwhelmed by the loyalty and enthusiasm of my Canadian people.

Also during 1957 my husband and I paid visits to Portugal, France, Denmark and the United States of America. In each case the arrangements and formalities were managed with great skill but no one could have 'managed' the welcome we received from the people.

In each country I was welcomed as Head of the Commonwealth and as your representative. These nations are our friends largely because we have always tried to do our best to be honest and kindly and because we have tried to stand up for what we believe to be right.

In the old days the monarch led his soldiers on the battlefield and his leadership at all times was close and personal.

Today things are very different. I cannot lead you into battle, I do not give you laws or administer justice but I can do something else, I can give you my heart and my devotion to these old islands and to all the peoples of our brotherhood of nations.

I believe in our qualities and in our strength, I believe that together we can set an example to the world which will encourage upright people everywhere.

I would like to read you a few lines from 'Pilgrim's Progress', because I am sure we can say with Mr Valiant for Truth, these words:

"Though with great difficulty I am got hither, yet now I do not repent me of all the trouble I have been at to arrive where I am. My sword I give to him that shall succeed me in my pilgrimage and my courage and skill to him that can get it. My marks and scars I carry with me, to be a witness for me that I have fought his battles who now will be my rewarder."

I hope that 1958 may bring you God's blessing and all the things you long for. And so I wish you all, young and old, wherever you may be, all the fun and enjoyment, and the peace of a very happy Christmas.

(The first televised Christmas broadcast, 1957 / *The Crown*, 2x05, min. 51:02)

The 1957 Christmas message was the first to be broadcast through television, and it was the sixth Christmas message by Queen Elizabeth since the beginning of her reign. As observed by Harrington et al. (2000), Harrington (2005) and Richards (2018), and as it was explored in Chapter 3, the Christmas broadcasts of the 1950s contain a higher frequency of U-RP features, and, if compared to those of 1980s and 1990s, a progressive accommodation of the Queen's pronunciation to the more modern features of Mainstream RP can be noticed. The scholars focused specifically on the quality of the Queen's vowel sounds, and they noticed, for example, that Her Majesty has been making a large use of the phenomenon of Happy-tensing in the last period of her reign (ibid.), while the first decades were marked by the generalised use of an open HAPPY vowel, whose realisation was between [ɪ] and [ɛ]. The acoustic analysis of the first televised Christmas message seems to confirm this observation, seeing that most of the words ending with a consonant followed by '-y' are pronounced with a final more open vowel sound than the more modern [i:]; some examples in the text are "family," "morality," "honesty," "amicably," "peacefully," "difficulty," "very" and "happy." Dialect coach William Conacher and actress Claire Foy apparently worked with particular care on the realisation of the aristocratic open HAPPY vowel, although Foy tends to keep it in the spectrum of the close-mid sounds, while the real Queen Elizabeth often used the open-mid [ɛ], especially with a few specific words such as "family" and "very."

The word 'very' as pronounced by the Queen in her young age contains almost always another traditional 'U' feature, namely the use of tapped-R in intervocalic position ([vɛɾɪ]). It is, in fact, especially in this phonological context that letter 'r' is pronounced by upper-class people as a vibrant, rather than a retroflex sound, for instance in words like "cherish," "America," "different" and "carry" in the text. In the fictional version of this speech, tapped-R is not much heard, except for a slight trace in "very" and in final position in "for" and "another." The adoption of a tap at the end of a word preceding one that starts with a vowel is heard only in the first case in the speech of the real Queen ("for a few minutes"), but not in the second ("another example"); in the same speech, she also used a tap in initial position once ("remote" [ɾɪməʊt]).

Another traditional phonological feature of U-RP that appears to be used very frequently by the Queen in this speech is the phenomenon of 'smoothing,' which is the name used by Wells (1998, 239) to refer to the process of reduction of some diphthongal sounds into monophthongs. Wells (ibid.) mentions that the diphthongs that are generally 'smoothed' in U-RP are the PRICE and MOUTH types, but, as it was explored in the analysis of the Queen's natural conversations in Chapter 3, other types of diphthongs are converted into single vowels by the monarch. In the 1957 Christmas message, in particular, the diphthong /eɪ/ in words like "day" and "today" is invariably realised as [e:]. A slight attempt by Foy to render this phenomenon in her version of this speech can be heard sporadically, and in general an emphasis on the first element of the diphthong is often added, but the sound seems to end almost always with the trace of a close vowel (i.e., 'day' [deːɪ]). Also, Foy pronounces the word 'really' with its standard mainstream /ɪə/ sound, while the real Queen Elizabeth, in this case, used the old-fashioned aristocratic pronunciation with a single mid vowel, thus resulting as [ɹeːlɪ] (see scene 7 in Chapter 3).

The following table sums up the comparison between the frequency of the three main U-RP features found in the first televised Christmas broadcast and its fictional version in *The Crown* through the use of percentages, which were calculated exclusively on the parts in bold in the text.

Table 7 – Frequency of U-RP features in Speech 1

[ɪ] in HAPPY		Tapped-R		'Smoothing'	
Original	Fiction	Original	Fiction	Original	Fiction
54 %	38 %	36 %	14 %	100 %	20 %

As shown in table 10, the fictional version contains a lower frequency of these U-RP features, with a greater discrepancy in the case of the 'smoothing' process, but, even though their use is less consistent than in the original version, their quality is generally well reproduced, thus providing this representation with a convincing level of realism and adherence to the model. Such adherence is also confirmed by the accurate realisation of other two 'U' vowels, which are [ɔ] instead of /ɒ/ in "God" and [ɛ] instead of /æ/ in "battles," and especially by the perfect prosodic rendition of the entire speech. The tone of the real young Elizabeth is sharper than Foy's timbre, but the actress achieved the same rhythm by mimicking an accurate stress pattern, and she generally uses the same high pitches and intonation. Her voice is also accurately laryngeal and, as regards supralaryngeal factors, her mouth is constantly as semi-closed as that of the real Queen, at times even more (the word 'broadcast,' for example, sounds even 'plummier' in Foy's case); additionally, the Queen's remarkable use of rounded lips in the word 'television' is perfectly rendered in the fictional version too. The following pitch marks and waveforms will help visualise the comparison between the prosodic aspects of the two versions of Speech 1.

Waveform 5 – The Queen's Christmas Broadcast 1957

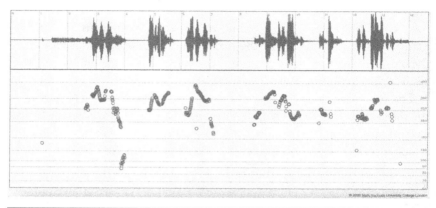

(Queen) And so I wish you all, young and old, wherever you may be, all the fun and enjoyment, and the peace of a very happy Christmas.

Waveform 6 – The Queen's Christmas Broadcast 1957, represented in *The Crown*, 2x05, 53:50

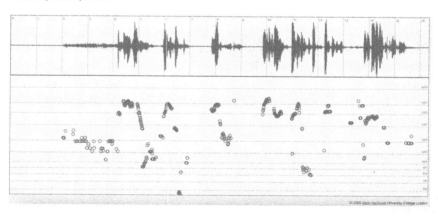

(Foy) And so I wish you all, young and old, wherever you may be, all the fun and enjoyment, and the peace of a very happy Christmas.

The two waveforms are very similar, both showing a remarkable amplitude, corresponding to a high level of intensity of the speech. The pitch marks show, on the other hand, a slight disparity in terms of variability: while the Queen's pitches are placed rather homogeneously in the upper part of the diagram, Foy's speech appears to be more oscillating. However, the actress's pitches are generally quite high, too, and the waves they design are very similar to those of the Queen's speech, thus confirming the accuracy of the fictional prosodic rendition.

The compared analysis of the two versions of Speech 1 focused exclusively on phonological and prosodic aspects, since the script is exactly the same and no relevant comments from the lexical and morphosyntactic point of view can be provided. However, it can be noted that the Queen uses the contraction "it's" twice (i.e., "It's inevitable" and "That it's possible") and, therefore, she shows a small trace of informality, whereas Foy has opted for the extended form, which is the one we find in the official transcription.

*

It would have been interesting to analyse a speech that the Queen delivered in the 1970s/1980s and compare it with its fictional version as rendered by actress Olivia Colman in seasons 3 or 4 of *The Crown*. Unfortunately, it was not possible to conduct such analysis, because recordings of the original versions of the few speeches represented in the last two seasons of the Netflix TV series are not available. There is one speech in season 4, however, whose official recording is easily found and can thus be analysed as a second text, despite not being reproduced by Colman in the series. Claire Foy, who played the role of Queen Elizabeth in the first two seasons, was in fact called back for a flashback scene, where the young Princess Elizabeth is shown reading a speech in the occasion of her 21st birthday to declare her complete dedication for a life to the service of the Commonwealth. This speech was delivered through radio broadcast in 1947 from Cape Town and it is represented in the eighth episode of the fourth season of *The Crown*. In this case, too, the official transcription[77] includes some parts in bold, which correspond to those read by Foy in the TV series.

---

77 This script was also taken from the official website of the Royal Family (https:// www.royal.uk/21st-birthday-speech-21-april-1947, last accessed 15/12/2020).

– Speech 2:

On my twenty-first birthday I welcome the opportunity to speak to all the peoples of the British Commonwealth and Empire, wherever they live, whatever race they come from, and whatever language they speak.

Let me begin by saying 'thank you' to all the thousands of kind people who have sent me messages of good will. This is a happy day for me; but it is also one that brings serious thoughts, thoughts of life looming ahead with all its challenges and with all its opportunity.

At such a time it is a great help to know that there are multitudes of friends all round the world who are thinking of me and who wish me well. I am grateful and I am deeply moved.

As I speak to you today from Cape Town, I am six thousand miles from the country where I was born. But I am certainly not six thousand miles from home. Everywhere I have travelled in these lovely lands of South Africa and Rhodesia my parents, my sister and I have been taken to the heart of their people and made to feel that we are just as much at home here as if we had lived among them all our lives.

That is the great privilege belonging to our place in the world-wide commonwealth – that there are homes ready to welcome us in every continent of the earth. Before I am much older I hope I shall come to know many of them.

Although there is none of my father's subjects from the oldest to the youngest whom I do not wish to greet, I am thinking especially today of all the young men and women who were born about the same time as myself and have grown up like me in terrible and glorious years of the second world war.

Will you, the youth of the British family of nations, let me speak on my birthday as your representative? Now that we are coming to manhood and womanhood it is surely a great joy to us all to think that we shall be able to take some of the burden off the shoulders of our elders who have fought and worked and suffered to protect our childhood.

We must not be daunted by the anxieties and hardships that the war has left behind for every nation of our commonwealth. We know that these things are the price we cheerfully undertook to pay for the high honour of standing alone, seven years ago, in defence of the liberty of the world. Let us say with Rupert Brooke: "Now God be thanked who has matched us with this hour."

I am sure that you will see our difficulties, in the light that I see them, as the great opportunity for you and me. Most of you have read in the history books the proud saying of William Pitt that England had saved herself by her exertions and would save Europe by her example. But in our time we may say that the British Empire has saved the world first, and has now to save itself after the battle is won.

I think that is an even finer thing than was done in the days of Pitt; and it is for us, who have grown up in these years of danger and glory, to see that it is accomplished in the long years of peace that we all hope stretch ahead.

If we all go forward together with an unwavering faith, a high courage, and a quiet heart, we shall be able to make of this ancient commonwealth, which we all love so dearly, an even grander thing – more free, more prosperous, more happy and a more powerful influence for good in the world – than it has been in the greatest days of our forefathers.

To accomplish that we must give nothing less than the whole of ourselves. There is a motto which has been borne by many of my ancestors – a noble motto, "I serve". Those words were an inspiration to many bygone heirs to the Throne when they made their knightly dedication as they came to manhood. I cannot do quite as they did.

But through the inventions of science I can do what was not possible for any of them. I can make my solemn act of dedication with a whole Empire listening. I should like to make that dedication now. It is very simple.

I declare before you all that my whole life whether it be long or short shall be devoted to your service and the service of our great imperial family to which we all belong.

But I shall not have strength to carry out this resolution alone unless you join in it with me, as I now invite you to do: I know that your support will be unfailingly given. God help me to make good my vow, and God bless all of you who are willing to share in it.

(Speech by the Queen on her 21st birthday, 1947 / *The Crown*, 4x08, min. 00:47)

Speech 2 was delivered ten years before Speech 1, and it dates back to five years before Elizabeth became queen. However, we hear it later than Speech 1 in *The Crown*, during a season in which Claire Foy was not part of the main cast any longer, and she was called back only to film this flashback. It is, therefore, interesting to observe if the fictional representation of this speech is as accurate as in the previous case, considering that at least three years had passed since the actress had left the series.

The correlation between the frequencies of the three main features that were examined previously in both versions is more or less the same here, that is quite balanced in the case of the open HAPPY vowel and a little more distant in the cases of tapped-R and the monophthongisation of /eɪ/. In this particular speech, however, there are some other U-RP features that stand out more, and one of these is the substitution of the diphthongal sound /aɪ/ with the long vowel [aː]. Instances of this phenomenon are found in the words "empire," "time," "price" and "science," which, on the contrary, are all pronounced with a regular /aɪ/ sound by Claire Foy. However, the 'smoothing' of the diphthong /aʊ/ in the words "town" and "now" (thus, [taːn] and [naː]) can be clearly heard in both real and fictional versions, but "vow" contains the same phenomenon only in the original speech.

Speech 2 is also characterised by the abundant use of other traditional U-RP vocalic features, such as [ɛ] in the TRAP lexical set (e.g., "language," "manhood," "grander," "that," in the text) and [ɔ] in CLOTH words (e.g., "continent," "Commonwealth," "off," "God," in the text); also, although not mentioned in the scholarly literature on the aristocratic accent, it is to be noted a raised vowel in THOUGHT, so that instances in the text like "fought," "all" and "short" are pronounced with a close-mid [o] sound rather than an open-mid /ɔ/. This general raising of monophthongs is retained and well reproduced in the episode of *The Crown*, as shown in Table 11 through the percentages.

Table 8 – Frequency of U-RP features in Speech 2

[ɛ] in TRAP		[ɔ] in CLOTH		[o] in THOUGHT		'Smoothing'	
Original	Fiction	Original	Fiction	Original	Fiction	Original	Fiction
63 %	50 %	100 %	100 %	100 %	100 %	100 %	29 %

In this case, too, the percentages are calculated exclusively on the bold parts of Speech 2, which correspond to the parts of the original speech that were reproduced in the TV series, and they show a noteworthy adherence of the fictional version to the original one in terms of rendition of the single vowel sounds. Therefore, it can be presumed that dialect coach Conacher identified the general raising of both front and back vowels as an indicator of upper-class language, and Claire Foy succeeded in reproducing this characteristic in most of the cases. Table 8 also shows, conversely, some inconsistency in the rendition of the diphthongal reduction, as it was observed in the analysis of Speech 1, too, but this is perfectly compensated by the extremely accurate voice quality and intonation of the actress, which she decidedly managed to maintain for all the episodes she appeared in. In light of the data that have just been discussed, it can be confirmed that Foy did not lose familiarity with the royal accent although she is no longer part of the main regular cast.

5.2. Other speeches

In order to expand the data resulting from the comparative analysis of the Queen's public speeches and their fictional versions, short parts of speeches by other members of the Royal Family (i.e., Prince Philip and Prince Charles) and the English aristocracy (i.e., Winston Churchill) will be examined in this section.[78]

The first speech is by Winston Churchill, who spoke to the Nation through radio broadcast on 7th February 1952 to announce the death of King George VI and the consequent beginning of Queen Elizabeth's reign. This speech by Winston Churchill well fits into the corpus of the texts to be analysed in this chapter, because he can certainly be considered a member of the upper class, being a direct descendant of John Churchill, first Duke of Marlborough. However, while this speech is reproduced in its extended version in the second episode of the first season of *The Crown*, only the following short part of the original version is available online:

– Speech 3:

> In the end, death came as a friend. And after a happy day of sunshine and sport, and after a goodnight to those who loved him best, he fell asleep, as every man or woman who strives to fear God and nothing else in the world may hope to do. I, whose youth was passed in the august, unchallenged and tranquil glories of the Victorian era, may well feel the thrill in invoking once more the prayer and the anthem "God Save the Queen."

(Speech by Churchill, 7th February 1947 / *The Crown*, 1x02, min. 56:38)

In this short passage of Churchill on the death of George VI, a few isolated features of U-RP can be detected, such as the reduction of the diphthong /eɪ/ in [e:] in the word "came," the use of [ɛ] instead of /æ/ in "unchallenged" and a remarkably open second element in the diphthong in "fear," pronounced as [fɪɑ:]. Also, a clear tap sound can be heard in the word "era." Upper-class features in Winston's oral language are more sporadic than in the Queen's speech, but he is fully perceived as an aristocrat thanks to his voice quality and intonation, which is characterised by numerous high

---

78 The short speeches found in this section were transcribed by me, with the help of the official Netflix subtitles.

pitches. This aspect is well rendered by actor John Lithgow,[79] who played the role of Churchill in *The Crown*, although from the phonological point of view he essentially used a mainstream form of RP.

Similar observations can be applied to the case of Prince Philip (Matt Smith in seasons 1 and 2). Unfortunately, it was not possible to select a full speech by the Duke of Edinburgh, but the following line, taken from the opening of the 1956 Summer Olympics in Melbourne, which was reproduced in episode 2x02 of *The Crown*, provides for a couple of elements to be briefly discussed.

– Speech 4:

> I declare open the Olympic Games of Melbourne, celebrating the 16th Olympiad of the modern era.
>
>   (Opening of 1956 Summer Olympics / *The Crown*, 2x02, min. 13:32)

As mentioned previously, the line is very short, and only two phonological aspects can be noticed: the use of a monophthong in "games" [ge:mz] and tapped-R in "era" [ɪərə]. Apart from reproducing a quite accurate prosody, Smith uses the so-called 'smoothing' of the diphthong /eɪ/, but his 'r' in "era" is not tapped. This observation supports the impression that the study of the upper-class accent on the set of *The Crown* was particularly focused on the rendition of the vocalic and the prosodic system, while the exact reproduction of consonants, such as the vibrant sounds – although it was not totally overlooked (see Speech 1 and 2, but also Chapter 4) – was arguably perceived as secondary, and perhaps too old-fashioned and stereo-typical, in the linguistic portrayal of noble figures. The same can be argued about seasons 3 and 4, taking as an example the reading style of Prince Charles (Josh O'Connor) in the following extracts. Speech 5 is the official oath of Charles during his investiture as Prince of Wales, reproduced during the sixth episode of the third season of *The Crown*, and Speech 6 is a short

---

79 No waveforms or pitch marks can be provided to show visually the prosodic similarity of the original and fictional speech in this case, because the scene in the episode of *The Crown* includes background noises produced by other characters and a background music, thus resulting in an overlap of different types of pitches.

part of a speech he delivered in Tasmania during his Commonwealth tour with Princess Diana in 1983, whose fictional version can be viewed in the sixth episode of season 4.

– Speech 5:

> I, Charles, Prince of Wales, to become your liege man of life and limb and of earthly worship and faith and truth, I will bear unto thee to live and die against all manner of folks.
>
> (Prince of Wales investiture, 1969 / *The Crown*, 3x06, min. 40:20)

– Speech 6:

> The last time I was here was two years ago, in 1981, and, at that time, everybody was saying "Good luck" and "Hope everything goes well" and "How lucky you are to be engaged to such a lovely lady". And, my goodness, I was lucky enough to marry her (*The Crown*: I am lucky enough to be married to her).
>
> (Prince of Wales in Tasmania, 1983 / *The Crown*, 4x06, min. 40:15)

In both original versions of these extracts, the main U-RP features are, alike Prince Philip's case, the monophthogisation of /eɪ/ in "Wales" [weːlz] and "lady" [leːdiː] and the use of a tap final sound in "bear" and "manner." These characteristics are not as marked in O'Connor's line, but it is again the aspect of voice quality that makes these speech representations extremely accurate. As mentioned in the previous chapter, in fact, O'Connor stood out in the series for his ability to maintain his mouth semi-closed and his teeth clenched in most scenes, thus succeeding in lowering his larynx and widening his oro-pharynx and, consequently, achieving that typical royal voice that Wells (1992, 283) calls 'plumminess.' At times, such quality of the voice is even more emphatic in O'Connor's case, who adopts a slower tone and a clearer articulation even when he reports what people have been telling him (e.g., "Hope everything goes well," etc, in Speech 6), whereas the real Charles arguably utters those sentences with a speaking rate, rather than an articulation rate (Thomas 2013, 119).

5.3. Final discussion

After examining the language of British upper-class people in face-to-face conversations, both in natural and audiovisual dialogue, this final chapter was specifically centred on the comparative side of the research. Both the original versions and the fictional reproductions in *The Crown* of two public speeches by Queen Elizabeth and some lines taken from speeches by Winston Churchill, Prince Philip and Prince Charles were analysed. All of them confirmed a noticeable adherence of the fictional versions to the original ones. More specifically, thanks to the gathered data, the following conclusions can be drawn:

- The representation of the upper-class accent in *The Crown* is rather accurate from the point of view of the vocalic system; Formant 1 of vowels, which is their height (Thomas 2013, 110), is generally well rendered: TRAP, CLOTH and THOUGHT words contain a closed sound, while in HAPPY a more open one than in Mainstream RP can be heard.
- A higher disparity is observed in the frequency of the so-called phenomenon of 'smoothing,' especially /eɪ/, which is reduced to [e:] only sporadically, although in the original versions this feature is heard almost in the totality of the FACE words in the text.
- The only consonantal feature of U-RP that can be heard in the original versions of the speeches that were analysed in this chapter is the use of tapped-R, mainly in intervocalic position, but also sparsely in initial and final position. Nowadays, this feature is considered to be old-fashioned even in aristocratic contexts, and the analysis of this chapter shows that it was in decline even in the 1950s and 1960s (see Ross 1959, who also mentions this), which is probably why it was used only very rarely by actors and actresses in *The Crown*. Moreover, the dialect coach of the series may have decided not to train the cast on the use of tapped-R because today it is often used in comedy shows to portray upper-class characters in a mocking and stereotypical way (see section 2.2.3).
- Suprasegmental phonology is definitely the most defining linguistic aspect of upper-class speech, and its reproduction in *The Crown* is extremely accurate; the cast's intonation, rhythm and voice quality are all very similar to their original counterparts. At times, the emphasis on the prosodic aspects is even more marked in the series than in reality, thus sounding more formal; yet, this overuse is so mild and sporadic that there is no risk for the dialogue in the series to be perceived as unrealistic.

Conclusions

This study was conceived as a descriptive contribution on the language of the British upper class, with the ambition of filling a gap in scholarly literature. As it was explored in the first part of the book, there are a few insights on the linguistic features of the language of the élite group in Britain, such as those by Ross (1954 and 1959) and Wells (1992), but they are not very recent. Britain (2017) and Fabricius (2018) have recently drawn the attention on the lack of a revisited study on the élite sociolect, which is due to the fact that it is still generally identified with the standard variety; both scholars argued that, although these two linguistic entities are undoubtedly related to one another, it must not be taken for granted that they are exactly the same, thus highlighting the need for particularised studies. They also affirm that the upper class should not be excluded from sample tests as it has often happened in the past.

Among the sparse recent insights related to the topic are the acoustic analyses to test the evolution of Queen Elizabeth's accent carried out by Harrington et al. (2000), Harrington (2005) and Richards (2018), who examined some of her public speeches between the 1950s and the 1990s, thus offering interesting data on the idiolect of one person. At present, there are no modern studies that deal explicitly with the language of the upper class in everyday face-to-face situations, despite the fact that the 'U' variety can be considered as a full enregistered variety, as argued by Agha (2007) and supported by Fabricius (2018). Ranzato (2018) offered a contribution on the presence of the upper-class accent in cinema and television and, therefore, showed that this variety is socially recognised and it is often exploited in fictional audiovisual dialogue for various aesthetic and narrative purposes.

Building on this scholarly literature, this study has tried to expand the discussion on upper-class English from multiple perspectives:

1) It provided a modern and revised description of the upper-class socio-lect by reorganising the sparse information on the language of the élite group detected in manuals of history of English, sociolinguistics and dialectology.

2) It offered original data from the acoustic analysis of the Queen's language in face-to-face spontaneous situations, which was accompanied by a brief overview on the language of the rest of the members of the Royal Family and some emblematic figures of the British nobility, such as the Mitford sisters.
3) It explored how the upper-class sociolect was rendered in the Netflix TV series *The Crown* (2016–present), or, more in general, how an accurate linguistic representation contributed in portraying an entire social class.
4) It offered an attentive comparison between U-RP in real life and U-RP in the fictional dialogue, thus helping discriminate between those features that are now stereotypical, or at least perceived as old-fashioned, and those that can be considered as indicators and markers of 'U' speech, to use Labov's terminology (1972).

Thanks to the qualitative analysis of the case studies, it is possible to draw the following conclusions on each one of the main features of upper-class English:[80]

- [ɛæ] or [ɛ] in TRAP: the raised sound in this lexical set was one of the main features of U-RP the 1950s/1960s, but the analysis of the case studies confirmed the outcomes by Harrington et al. (2000) on the decline of this phenomenon in favour of a progressive use of the more mainstream /æ/. The frequency of the traditional form is quite high in public speeches delivered by the members of the Royal Family at the beginning of Elizabeth's reign (see Chapter 5), while its use is rather sporadic in recent conversational speech (see Chapter 3). In *The Crown*, an occasional use of [ɛ] in TRAP is heard in seasons 1 and 2, and it becomes sporadic in seasons 3 and 4 (see Chapter 4), thus confirming that it can be considered as a marker of U-RP whose frequency has been in decline since the middle of the twentieth century.
- [ɪ] or [ɛ] in HAPPY: the evolution of this feature is more or less similar to that of the previous one; the results of the qualitative analysis of this study confirm the scholarly literature on the decline of mid vowels

---

80 The list is based primarily on Wells's taxonomy (1992), and partially on Ross's (1959), but some features are original outcomes of this study, as it is indicated in the text.

at the end of HAPPY in favour of a more modern [i:]. In this case, too, a higher frequency of this feature is noted in the language of public speeches, both in natural and audiovisual dialogue, while in conversational style it is rather sporadic and confined to a few specific words, such as 'very' and 'family,' or to add some emphasis at the end of an utterance. Despite the decline of this feature, in fact, upper-class speakers are arguably more conscious about its significance, compared to that of the TRAP vowel, and there are also instances of stereotypical parodies of aristocratic people where the final [ɪ] is clearly emphasised (see section 2.2.3).

- **Tapped-R:** the vibrant sound in intervocalic position is another traditional feature of U-RP that is less heard nowadays; however, in this case, more than a decline in the language of single speakers, it is to be considered as a characteristic of the language of the older generation which has not been passed on the younger generations. Queen Elizabeth, for example, has always used it sporadically but consistently, both in conversations and in reading style. In *The Crown*, it is used with the same moderate frequency only in the lines of the older characters (Elizabeth, her mother and her grandmother, Mr and Mrs Churchill). Also, as in the case of the HAPPY vowel, tapped-R is often overused in parodic representations of upper-class people, therefore it can be considered as a stereotype in a Labovian sense (1966/2006).

- **'Smoothing':** both Ross (1959) and Wells (1992) mention the phenomenon of the monophthongisation in MOUTH and PRICE as a secondary peculiarity of upper-class speech; however, not only do the results of this study show that it is extremely frequent, but the same phenomenon applies to FACE words too. Diphthongs /aʊ, aɪ, eɪ/ are pronounced respectively as [a:, a:, e:] in most cases in the natural dialogue, both in conversations and in public speeches, while the same frequency is not always found in the audiovisual text. In both versions, the feature is perhaps used more by female speakers.

- **[ɔ] in CLOTH:** the substitution of /ɒ/ with [ɔ] in the CLOTH lexical set resulted to be the most frequent phenomenon in U-RP. It is heard almost in the totality of the occurrences in all the excerpts that were analysed in this volume: both in real and fictional language, both in conversational and reading style, both in older and more recent recordings, both in female and male speech.

- **[o] in THOUGHT:** although this feature is not mentioned in scholarly literature on the accent of the upper-class, it was observed through the analysis of the case studies in this study that it is not uncommon to hear aristocratic people using it. This phenomenon is perhaps a consequence of the use of [ɔ] in CLOTH, to differentiate the two lexical sets, and it is occasionally found in the utterances of all kinds of speakers (male and female, real and fictional).
- **[ɪn] variant:** considered as an old-fashioned feature by Wells (1992), this characteristic is only sporadically noted in the old recordings of Queen Elizabeth and in the first two seasons of *The Crown*, mainly by women.
- **Laryngeal voice quality:** the so-called 'plumminess' (Wells 1992) is by all means the most recognisable characteristic of the language of upper-class people in Britain. All the real people and fictional characters analysed in this study speak with this type of voice, produced by the lowering of the larynx and the opening of the oro-pharynx. As it was observed in Chapters 4 and 5, this phenomenon is affected by several actors and actresses in *The Crown* by speaking with a semi-closed mouth.
- **High-pitched intonation:** thanks to the waveforms generated with the WASP programme, it was possible to observe that the utterances by upper-class members present frequent high pitches, and this aspect was accurately rendered in the audiovisual representation too.
- **Rounded lips:** this supralaryngeal factor was not mentioned by Wells (1992) or any other scholar, but it was occasionally noticed during the acoustic analysis of the case studies in this book. The use of rounded lips is apparently often combined with the utterance of the affricate sound /tʃ/ in initial position (e.g., in 'children') and the fricative /ʃ/ in nouns ending in '-tion;' it is arguably found more frequently in female speakers. It would be interesting to carry out a systematic quantitative analysis to measure the occurrences of this factor in upper-class language.

Moreover, a few observations from the lexical point of view can be added. First of all, the analysis confirmed Phillipps's discussion (1984) on the fact that upper-class language is not free from informal words and expressions, although the use of slang is generally confined to the spoken language of men. Also, upper-class English is not always synonym of correctness and accuracy (ibid.): instances of vague expressions, discourse fillers and contractions are frequently found in natural aristocratic language (see Chapter 3); on the contrary, this aspect was not always rendered fictionally in *The Crown*, where the discourse is generally rather fluid in conversations (see Chapter 4), and free from informalities, such as contractions, in public speeches, even when they are present in the original version (see Chapter 5). The audiovisual representation, however, accurately debunked the myth of the upper-class usage of expressions that sound 'posh' or cultivated, such as French loans and euphemisms; contrarily to popular belief, in fact, the élite group favours a direct language, so much so that they never use, for instance, 'pardon/ I beg your pardon' and they simply use 'what?' or 'sorry.'

After Ross (1959), no other scholar focused on upper-class vocabulary in everyday face-to-face language, and this research could only show sporadic original insights on this topic, also building on recent non-academic literature (Fox 2004; Taggart 2010; Hanson 2017), which, at any rate, might be used as a starting point for a methodical sociolinguistic on-field research. The main limitation of this study, in fact, was the impossibility to conduct an investigation through sample tests and qualitative interviews, but these tools would certainly provide for useful data to expand the critical description of the 'U' sociolect in every linguistic aspect. Perception studies could also be explored as a further step in this research, for what concerns both natural and audiovisual dialogue, in order to offer a more complete view on the definition of British upper-class English, which is rarely explicitly explored, although it is unmistakably recognisable (Waugh 1959).

Bibliography

Abbink, Jon, and Tijo Salverda, eds. 2013. *The Anthropology of Elites: Power, Culture, and the Complexities of Distinction*. London: Palgrave Macmillan.

Abbiss, Will Stanford. 2020. "Heritage and Post-Heritage: Investigating the Style, Form and Genre of Period Drama in 2010s British Television." PhD diss., Victoria University of Wellington.

Agha, Asif. 2003. "The social life of cultural value." *Language & Communication* 23: 231–273.

Agha, Asif. 2007. *Language and Social Relations*. Cambridge: Cambridge University Press.

Aitken, A. J. 1984. "Scots and English in Scotland." In *Language in the British Isles*, edited by Peter Trudgill, 517–532. Cambridge: Cambridge University Press.

Altendorf, Ulrike. 2003 *Estuary English: Levelling at the Interface of RP and South-Eastern British English*. Tübingen: Gunter Narr Verlag.

Arkin, Daniel. 2020. "Netflix Needs to Make Clear *The Crown* is Fictional, British Culture Minister Says." *NBC News*, November 30, 2020. https://www.nbcnews.com/pop-culture/tv/netflix-needs-make-clear-crown-fictional-british-culture-minister-says-n1249397.

Armstrong, Nigel, and Federico M. Federici, eds. 2006. *Translating Voices, Translating Regions*. Rome: Aracne.

Badia Barrera, Berta. 2015. "A Sociolinguistic Study of T-Glottaling in Young RP: Accent, Class and Education." PhD diss., University of Essex.

Baños Piñero, Rocío, and Frederic Chaume. 2009. "Prefabricated Orality: A Challenge in Audiovisual Translation." *The Translation of Dialects in Multimedia*. Special Issue of *inTRAlinea*, edited by Giorgio Marrano, Giovanni Nadiani, and Christopher Rundle. http://www.intralinea.org/specials/article/1714.

Barry, Ellen. 2018. "It's the Ultimate TV Prize: An Unscripted Queen Elizabeth." *The New York Times*, January 14, 2018. https://www.nytimes.com/2018/01/14/arts/television/queen-coronation-bbc-smithsonian.html.

Bastin, Giselle. 2009. "Filming the Ineffable: Biopics of the British Royal Family." *Auto/Biography Studies* 24, no. 1 (Summer): 34–52.

Bastin, Giselle. 2020. "Friday Essay: The Hidden Agenda of Royal Experts Circling *The Crown* Series 4." *The Conversation*, December 10, 2020. https://theconversation.com/friday-essay-the-hidden-agenda-of-royal-experts-circling-the-crown-series-4-151293.

Baugh, Albert C., and Thomas Cable. 2013. *A History of the English Language*. London/New York: Routledge.

Beal, Joan. 2010. *An Introduction to Regional Englishes*. Edinburgh: Edinburgh University Press.

Beal, Joan. 2020. "A Received Pronunciation: Eighteenth-Century Pronouncing Dictionaries and the Precursors of RP." In *Late Modern English: Novel Encounters*, edited by Merja Kytö and Erik Smitterberg, 22–41. Amsterdam: John Benjamins.

Bell, Allan. 1984. "Language Style as Audience Design." *Language in Society* 13 (2): 145–204.

Bell, Allan, 1997, "Language Style as Audience Design." In *Sociolinguistics: A Reader and Coursebook*, edited by Nikolas Coupland and Adam Jaworski, 240–250. Basingstoke/London: MacMillan.

Bell, Matthew. 2018. "U and Non-U: How to Be Upper Class in 2019." *Tatler*, December 5, 2018. https://www.tatler.com/article/nancy-mitford-u-and-non-u-language.

Berruto, Gaetano. 2003. *Fondamenti di Sociolinguistica*. Rome: Laterza.

Block, David. 2014. *Social Class in Applied Linguistics*. London/ New York: Routledge.

Bondebjerg, Ib. 2020. *Screening Twentieth Century Europe: Television, History, Memory*. Houndmills: Palgrave Macmillan.

Brenner, Koloman, and Irmeli Helin, eds. 2016. *The Translation of Dialects in Multimedia III*. Special Issue of *inTRAlinea*. http://www.intralinea.org/specials/article/2205.

Britain, David. 2017. "Beyond the 'Gentry Aesthetic': Elites, Received Pronunciation and the Dialectological Gaze." *Social Semiotics* 27 (3): 288–298. DOI: 10.1080/10350330.2017.1301794.

Brook, George Leslie. 1976. *The Language of Dickens*. London: Andre Deutsch.

Bruti, Silvia, and Gianmarco Vignozzi. 2016. "Voices from the Anglo-Saxon World: Accents and Dialects Across Film Genres." *Status Quaestionis* 11: 42–74. DOI: 10.13133/2239-1983/13832.

Bryman, Alan. 2012. *Social Research Methods*. Oxford: Oxford University Press.

Buckle, Richard. 1978. *U and Non-U Revisited*. London: Debrett's Peerage.

Buizza, Emanuela, and Leendert Plug. 2012. "Lenition, Fortition and the Status of Plosive Affrication: The Case of Spontaneous RP English /t/." *Phonology* 29 (1): 1–38.

Care, Christina. No date. "Perfecting Accent Work with Dialect Coach William Conacher." *Spotlight: The Home of Casting*. https://www. spotlight.com/news-and-advice/interviews-podcasts/perfecting-accent-work-with-dialect-coach-william-conacher/.

Chambers, Jack. 2003. *Sociolinguistic Theory: Linguistic Variation and its Social Significance*. London: John Wiley.

Chesire, Jennifer, and Viv Edwards. 1993. "Sociolinguistics in the Classroom: Exploring Linguistic Diversity." In *Real English: The Grammar of English Dialect in the British Isles*, edited by James Milroy and Leslie Milroy, 34–51. London/New York: Longman.

Chesterman, Andrew. 1997. *Memes of Translation*. Amsterdam: John Benjamins.

Chiaro, Delia. 2008. "Where Have All the Varieties Gone? The Vicious Circle of the Dis-appearance Act in Screen Translations." In *Dialect for All Seasons*, edited by Irmeli Helin, 9–25. München: Nodus.

Clyne, Michaerl G. 2004. "Pluricentric Language." In *Sociolinguistics: An International Handbook of the Science of Language and Society* (vol.1), edited by Ulrich Ammon, Norbert Dittmar, Klaus J. Mattheier, and Peter Trudgill, 296–300. Berlin: Walter de Gruyter.

Coggle, Paul. 1993. *Do You Speak Estuary?: The New Standard English*. London: Bloomsbury.

Copping, Jasper. 2012. "Prince William's Cut-glass Accent is a Little Less Polished than Kate Middleton's." *The Telegraph*, November 4, 2012. https://www.telegraph.co.uk/news/newstopics/howaboutthat/9653166/Prince-Williams-cut-glass-accent-is-a-little-less-polished-than-Kate-Middletons.html.

Coşeriu, Eugen. 1969. *Einführung in die Strukturelle Linguistik: Vorlesung gehalten im Winter-Semester 1967/68 an der Universität Tübingen.* Tübingen: University of Tübingen.

Coupland, Nikolas. 2007. *Style: Language Variation, and Identity.* Cambridge: Cambridge University Press.

Cruttenden, Alan. 1994/2014. *Gimson's Pronunciation of English.* London/ New York: Routledge.

Crystal, David. 1995/2000. *The Cambridge Encyclopedia of the English Language.* Cambridge: Cambridge University Press.

Crystal, David. 2010. "Language Developments in British English." In *The Cambridge Companion to Modern British Culture*, edited by Michael Higgins, Clarissa Smith, and John Storey, 26–41. Cambridge: Cambridge University Press.

Cunningham, Niall, and Mike Savage. 2015. "The Secret Garden? Elite Metropolitan Geographies in the Contemporary UK." *Sociological Review* 63 (2): 321–348.

Dawkins, Richard. 1976. *The Selfish Gene.* Oxford: Oxford University Press.

De Pascale, Carla. 2013. "From Received Pronunciation to Estuary English: A Shift from Diastratic Variation." PhD diss., University of Salerno.

Denison, David. 1998. "Syntax." In *The Cambridge History of the English Language: 1776–Present-day* (vol. IV), edited by Suzanne Romaine, 92–329. Cambridge: Cambridge University Press.

Devonshire, Deborah. 2010. *Wait for me! Memoirs of the Youngest Mitford Sister.* London: John Murray.

Di Giovanni, Elena, Francesca Diodati, and Giorgia Franchini. 1994. "Il Problema delle Varietà Linguistiche nella Traduzione Filmica." In *Il doppiaggio: Trasposizioni Linguistiche e Culturali*, edited by Rosa Maria Bollettieri Bosinelli, Laura Gavioli, and Raffaella Baccolini, 99–104. Bologna: CLUEB.

Di Giovanni, Elena. 2003. "Cultural Otherness and Global Communication in Walt Disney Films at the Turn of the Century." *The Translator* 9: 207–223.

Di Martino, Emilia. 2012. "When the Same Book Speaks Two Different Languages: Identity and Social Relationships Across Cultures in the Italian Translation of *The Uncommon Reader.*" *Anglistica* 16. 1–2: 57–83.

Di Martino, Emilia. 2019. *Celebrity Accents and Public Identity Construction*. London/New York: Routledge.

Ellis, Alexander. 1869. *On Early English Pronunciation*. Cambridge: Philological Society.

Fabricius, Anne H. 2000. "T-Glottaling: Between Stigma and Prestige: A Sociolinguistic Study of Modern RP." PhD diss., Copenhagen Business School.

Fabricius, Anne H. 2007. "Variation and Change in the TRAP and STRUT Vowels of RP: A Real Time Comparison of the Five Acoustic Data Sets." *Journal of the International Phonetic Association* 37: 293–320. https://doi.org/10.1017/S002510030700312X.

Fabricius, Anne H. 2018. "Social Change, Linguistic Change and Sociolinguistic Change in Received Pronunciation." In *Sociolinguistics in England*, edited by Natalie Braber and Sandra Jansen, 35–66. London: Palgrave Macmillan.

Federici, Federico M., ed. 2009. *Translating Regionalised Voices in Audiovisuals*. Rome: Aracne.

Ferguson, Emily. 2020. "Princess Charlotte Speaks Queen's English but George and Louis have more unusual accents." *Express*, October 9, 2020. https://www.express.co.uk/news/royal/1345092/princess-charlotte-news-prince-george-prince-louis-queens-english-accents-video.

Fleming, Peter. 1959. "Posh Lingo." In *Noblesse Oblige*, edited by Nancy Mitford, 123–138. Oxford: Oxford University Press.

Flydal, Leiv. 1952. "Remarques sur Certains Rapports entre le Style et l'État de Langue." *Norsk Tidsskrift for Sprogvidenskap* 16: 241–258.

Fox, Kate. 2004. *Watching the English. The Hidden Rules of English Behaviour*. London: Hodder & Stoughton.

Geyer, Klaus, and Margherita Dore, eds. 2020. *The Translation of Dialects in Multimedia IV*. Special Issue of *inTRAlinea*. http://www.intralinea.org/specials/article/2467.

Giles, Howard. 1970. "Evaluative Reactions to Accents." *Educational Review* 23: 211–227.

Giles, Howard. 1971. "Patterns of Evaluation in Reactions to RP, South Welsh and Somerset Accented Speech." *British Journal of Social and Clinical Psychology* 10.3: 280–281.

Gillet, Francesca. 2019. "Has Meghan's Accent Changed Since Marrying Prince Harry?" *BBC News*, February 27, 2019. https://www.bbc.com/news/uk-47148541.

Gimson, Alfred C. 1984. "The RP Accent." In *Language in the British Isles*, edited by Peter Trudgill, 45–54. Cambridge: Cambridge University Press.

Goodman, Sharon. 1997. " 'One' and the Pun: How Newspapers Keep the Monarchy in Its Place." *Language and Literature: Journal of the Poetics and Linguistic Association* 6 (3): 197–209.

Görlach, Manfred. 1999. *English in Nineteenth-Century England: An Introduction*. Cambridge: Cambridge University Press.

Gregory, Michael, and Susanne Carroll. 1978. *Language and Situation. Language Varieties and Their Social Contexts*. London/New York: Routledge.

Hallam, Julia, and Margaret Marshment. 2000. *Realism and Popular Cinema*. Manchester: Manchester University Press.

Halliday, Michael A. K. 1978. *Language as Social Semiotic: The Interpretation of Language and Meaning*. London: Edward Arnold.

Hanson, William. 2014. *The Bluffer's Guide to Etiquette*. Sparkford: Haynes Publishing.

Hanson, William. 2017. "U and Non-U: Does Anyone Still Care?" *BBC Radio 4*. Podcast. https://www.bbc.co.uk/programmes/b091w2p4.

Hanson, William. 2017. "Ten Words That Prove You Aren't Posh." *BBC Radio 4*. https://www.bbc.co.uk/programmes/articles/3qF356d7d2D6h98-CdCWxf8z/ten-words-that-prove-you-arent-posh.

Harrington, Jonathan. 2006. "An Acoustic Analysis of 'Happy-Tensing' in the Queen's Christmas Broadcasts." *Journal of Phonetics* 34: 439–457.

Harrington, Jonathan, Sallyanne Palethorpe, and Catherine Watson. 2000. "Monophthongal Vowel Changes in Received Pronunciation: An Acoustic Analysis of the Queen's Christmas Broadcasts." *Journal of the International Phonetic Association* 30 (1/2): 63–78.

Harvey, Keith. 1998. "Compensation." In *Routledge Encyclopedia of Translation Studies*, edited by Mona Baker and Kirsten Malmkjæ, 37–39. London/New York: Routledge.

Hayes, Lydia. 2020. "An Interdisciplinary Approach to Studying Linguistic Variation in Audiovisual Texts: Extrapolating a Synergy of Neuropsychology, Semiotics, Permormativity, and Memetics to Translation Studies." *Syn-Thèses* 9–10: 90–107.

Hernández-Campoy, Juan M. 2016. *Sociolinguistic Styles*. Oxford: Blackwell.

Hernández-Campoy, Juan M., and Juan Antonio Cutillas-Espinosa. 2012. *Style-Shifting in Public: New Perspectives on Stylistic Variation*. Amsterdam/Philadelphia: John Benjamins.

Hervey, Sándor, and Ian Higgins. 1992. *Thinking Translation. A Course in Translation Method: French-English*. London/New York: Routledge.

Hickey, Raymond. 2012. "Standard Irish English." In *Standards of English: Codified Varieties Around the World*, edited by Raymond Hickey, 96–116. Cambridge: Cambridge University Press.

Hinton, Martin. 2015. "Changes in Received Pronunciation: Diachronic Case Studies." *Research in Language* 13, no. 1: 21–37. DOI: 10.1515/rela-2015-0010.

Hodson, Jane. 2014. *Dialect in Film and Literature*. Houndmills: Palgrave MacMillan.

Honey, John. 1989. *Does Accent Matter? The Pygmalion Factor*. London: Faber and Faber.

Horton, Adrian. 2019. "Telling Porkies: No, Peppa Pig is not Giving American Kids British Accents." *The Guardian*, February 14, 2019. https://www.theguardian.com/tv-and-radio/2019/feb/14/peppa-pig-american-children-british-accents.

Hymes, Dell H. 1974. "Ways of Speaking." In *Explorations in the Ethnography of Speaking*, edited by Richard Bauman and Joel Sherzer, 433–451. Cambridge: Cambridge University Press.

Iaia, Pietro Luigi. 2018. "The Representation of Foreign Speakers in TV Series: Ideological Influence of the Linguacultural Background on Source and Target Scripts." In *Linguistic and Cultural Representation in Audiovisual*, edited by Irene Ranzato and Serenella Zanotti, 147–162. London/New York: Routldege.

Ingham, Richard. 2012. *The Transmission of Anglo-Norman: Language History and Language Acquisition*. Amsterdam/Philadelphia: John Benjamins Publishing.

Jaeckle, Jeff. 2013. *Film Dialogue*. London/New York: Wallflower Press.

Jenkins, Simon. 2020. "*The Crown*'s Fake History is as Corrosive as Fake News." *The Guardian*, November 16, 2020. https://www.theguardian.com/commentisfree/2020/nov/16/the-crown-fake-history-news-tv-series-royal-family-artistic-licence.

Kerswill, Paul. 2007. "Standard and Non-Standard English." In *Language in the British Isles*, edited by David Britain, 34–51. Cambridge: Cambridge University Press.

Khan, Shamus Rahman. 2012. "The Sociology of Elites." *Annual Review of Sociology* 38: 361–377.

Kroch, Anthony. 1996. "Dialect and Style in the Speech of Upper-Class Philadelphia." In *Towards a Social Science of Language: Papers in Honor of William Labov*, edited by Gregory R. Guy, Crawford Feagin, Deborah Schiffrin, and John Baugh, 23–45. Amsterdam/Phildadelphia: John Benjamins.

Labov, William. 1963. "The Social Motivation of a Sound Change." *Word* 19: 273–309.

Labov, William. 1966/2006. *The Social Stratification of English in New York City*. Cambridge: Cambridge University Press.

Labov, William. 1972. *Sociolinguistic Patterns*. Philadelphia: University of Philadelphia Press.

Laneri, Raquel. 2017. "How Claire Foy Perfected the Queen's English for *The Crown*." *New York Post*, December 7, 2017. https://nypost.com/2017/12/07/how-claire-foy-perfected-the-queens-english-for-the-crown/.

Leith, Dick. 2005. *A Social History of English*. London/New York: Routledge.

Lieb, Hans-Heinrich. 1993. *Linguistic Variables: Towards a Unified Theory of Linguistic Variation*. Amsterdam/Philadelphia: John Benjamins.

Lippi-Green, Rosina. 2012. *English with an Accent: Language, Ideology, and Discrimination in the United States*. London/ New York: Routledge.

Liwag Dixon, Christine-Marie. 2020. "Expert Explains What Prince Harry's Shifting Accent Really Means." *The List*, September 8, 2020. https://www.thelist.com/244544/expert-explains-what-prince-harrys-shifting-accent-really-means/.

Lohr, Steve. 1992. "On Language: The Accent Gap." *The New York Times*, August 23, 1992. https://www.nytimes.com/1992/08/23/magazine/on-language-the-accent-gap.html.

Lovell, Mary S. 2001. *The Sisters: The Saga of the Mitford Family*. New York/ London: W.W. Norton & Company.

Macauley, Ronald K. S. 1977. *Language, Social Class, and Education: A Glasgow Study*. Edinburgh: Edinburgh University Press.

Mangan, Lucy. 2018. "The Coronation Review – Queen Shines in a Surprisingly Fun Royal Coup." *The Guardian*, January 15, 2018. https://www.theguardian.com/tv-and-radio/2018/jan/14/the-coronation-queen-shines-in-a-surprisingly-fun-royal-coup.

Marrano, Giorgio, Giovanni Nadiani, and Christopher Rundle, eds. 2009. *The Translation of Dialects in Multimedia*. Special Issue of *inTRAlinea*. http://www.intralinea.org/specials/article/1720.

Mason, Ian. 1997. "Politeness in Screen Translating." In *The Translator as Communicator*, edited by Basil Hatim and Ian Mason, 78–96. London/New York: Routledge.

McCafferty, Kevin. 2007. "Northern Irish English." In *Language in the British Isles*, edited by David Britain, 122–134. Cambridge: Cambridge University Press.

Meares, Hadley. 2019. "The 1969 Documentary That Tried to Humanize Queen Elizabeth II and the Royal Family." *History*, November 19, 2019. https://www.history.com/news/queen-elizabeth-ii-1969-royal-family-documentary.

Mesthrie, Rajend, Joan Swann, Ana Deumert, and William L. Leap. 2009. *Introducing Sociolinguistics*. Edinburgh: Edinburgh University Press.

Meyerhoff, Miriam, and Anna Strycharz. 2013. "Communities of Practice." In *The Handbook of Language Variation and Change*, edited by Jack Chambers and Natalie Schilling, 428–447. Oxford: Blackwell.

Milroy, James, and Lesley Milroy. 1978. "Belfast: Change and Variation in an Urban Vernacular." In *Sociolinguistic Patterns in British English*, edited by Peter Trudgill, 19–36. London: E.Arnold.

Milroy, James, and Lesley Milroy. 1997. "Varieties and Variation." In *The Handbook of Sociolinguistics*, edited by Florian Coulmas, 47–121. Oxford: Blackwell.

Milroy, James, and Lesley Milroy. 2002. *Authority in Language*. London/New York: Routledge.

Milroy, James. 2001. "Received Pronunciation: Who 'Receives' it and How Long Will it Be 'Received'?" *Studia Anglia Posnaniensia* 36: 15–34.

Milroy, Lesley, and Carmen Llamas. 2013. "Social Networks." In *The Handbook of Language Variation and Change*, edited by Jack Chambers and Natalie Schilling, 409–427. Oxford: Blackwell.

Mitford, Nancy. 1945. *The Pursuit of Love*. Harmondsworth: Penguin Books.

Mitford, Nancy, ed. 1959. *Noblesse Oblige: An Enquiry Into the Identifiable Characteristics of the English Aristocracy*. Oxford: Oxford University Press.

Monk, Claire. 2001. "Sexuality and Heritage." In *Literature/Film/Heritage: A Sight and Sound Reader*, edited by Ginette Vincendeau, 6–11. London: BFI Publishing.

Morrish, John. 1999. "The Accent That Dare Not Speak its Name." *The Independent*, March 21, 1999. https://www.phon.ucl.ac.uk/home/estuary/morrish.htm.

Mosley, Charlotte. 2007. *The Mitfords: Letters Between Six Sisters*. New York: Harper Collins.

Mugglestone, Lynda. 2007. *Talking Proper. The Rise and Fall of the English Accent as a Social Symbol*. Oxford: Oxford University Press.

Mugglestone, Lynda. 2017. "Received Pronunciation." In *The History of English: Varieties of English*, edited by Alexander Bergs and Laurel Brinton, 151–168. Berlin: De Gruyter Mouton.

Munday, Jeremy. 2009. *The Routledge Companion to Translation Studies*. London/New York: Routledge.

Nadiani, Giovanni, and Chris Rundle, eds. 2012. *The Translation of Dialects in Multimedia II*. Special Issue of *inTRAlinea*. http://www.intralinea.org/specials/article/1851.

Nevalainen, Terttu. 2006. *An Introduction to Early Modern English*. Edinburgh: Edinburgh University Press.

Noonan, Peggy. 2017. "The lies of *The Crown* and *The Post*." *Wall Street Journal*, December 28, 2017. https://www.wsj.com/articles/the-lies-of-the-crown-and-the-post-1514505833.

"Pardon? That's practically a swear word." *The Lady*. https://lady.co.uk/pardon-thats-practically-swear-word.

Pavesi, Maria. 1994. "Osservazioni sulla (Socio)Linguistica del Doppiaggio." In *Il Doppiaggio: Trasposizioni Linguistiche e Culturali*, edited by Rosa Maria Bollettieri Bosinelli, Laura Gavioli, and Raffaella Baccolini, 129–142. Bologna: CLUEB.

Pearson, Roberta. 2021. "The Biggest Drama Commission in British Television History: Netflix, *The Crown*, and the UK Television Ecosystem." In *A European Television Fiction Renaissance: Premium*

Production Models and Transnational Circulation, edited by Luca Barra and Massimo Scaglioni. London/New York: Routledge.

"Peppa Pig Making American Children Speak with English Accents, Parents Claim." *The Independent*, February 13, 2019. https://www.independent. co.uk/arts-entertainment/tv/news/peppa-pig-children-american-english-accent-cartoon-network-a8777581.html.

Pérez-González, Luis. 2014. *Audiovisual Translation: Theories, Methods and Issues*. London/New York: Routledge.

Phillipps, Kenneth C. 1985. *Language and Class in Victorian England*. Oxford: Blackwell.

Preston, Dennis. 2002. "Language with an Attitude." In *The Handbook of Language Variation and Change*, edited by J.K. Chambers, Peter Trudgill and Natalie Schilling Estes, 40–66. Oxford: Blackwell.

Przedlacka, Joanna. 2002. "Estuary English and RP: Some Recent Findings." *Studia Anglica Posnaniensia* 36: 35–50.

Ramsaran, Susan. 1990. "RP: fact and fiction." In *Studies in the Pronunciation of English: A Commemorative Volume in Honour of A.C. Gimson*, edited by Susan Ramsaran, 178–190. London: Routledge.

Ranzato, Irene. 2006. "Tradurre Dialetti e Socioletti nel Cinema e nella Televisione." In *Translating Voices, Translating Regions*, edited by Nigel Armstrong and Federico M. Federici, 142–159. Rome: Aracne.

Ranzato, Irene. 2017. *'Queen's English?' Gli accenti dell'Inghilterra*. Rome: Bulzoni Editore.

Ranzato, Irene. 2018. "The British upper classes: Phonological fact and screen fiction." In *Linguistic and Cultural Representation in Audiovisual Translation*, edited by Irene Ranzato and Serenella Zanotti, 203–227. London/New York: Routledge.

Ranzato, Irene. 2019. "The Cockney Persona: The London Accent in Characterisation and Translation." *Perspectives* 27 (2): 235–251. DOI: 10.1080/0907676X.2018.1532442.

Ranzato, Irene. 2021. "An Audiovisual Topos: The 'Butler' Character." *Textus* 34 (1): 181–201.

Ranzato, Irene et al. 2017. *Dialects in Audiovisuals*. https://dialectsinav. wixsite.com/home/.

Richards, Lorna. 2018. "Lifting the Lid on the Queen's Upper-crust Received Pronunciation." *Leviathan: Interdisciplinary Journal in English* 3: 51–65.

Richardson, Kay. 2010. *Television Dramatic Dialogue: A Sociolinguistic Study*. Oxford: Oxford University Press.

Rieden, Juliet. 2019. "The True Story of the Royal Family's BBC Documentary, Which Hasn't Been Seen Publicly in Decades." *Town & Country*, November 23, 2019. https://www.townandcountrymag.com/society/tradition/a29686896/royal-family-1969-bbc-documentary/.

Roach, Peter. 2004. "British English: Received Pronunciation." *Journal of the International Phonetic Association* 34 (2): 239–245.

Roach, Peter, Gerry Knowles, Tamas Varadi, and Simon Arnfield. 1994. "MARSEC: A Machine-Readable Spoken English Corpus." *Journal of the International Phonetic Association* 23: 47–54.

Roche, Elisa. 2012. "Tragedy and Despair Behind Miranda Hart's Rise to the Top." *The Daily Express*, February 16, 2012. https://www.express.co.uk/celebrity-news/302418/Tragedy-and-despair-behind-Miranda-Hart-s-rise-to-the-top.

Romain, Suzanne. 2000. *Language in Society: An Introduction to Sociolinguistics*. Oxford: Oxford University Press.

Rose, David, and David Pevalin. 2003. *A Researcher's Guide to the National Statistics Socio-Economic Classification*. London: Sage.

Rosewarne, David. 1984. "Estuary English." *Times Educational Supplement* 29.

Rosewarne, David. 1994. "Estuary English: Tomorrow's RP?" *English Today* 37. 10 (1): 3–8.

Ross, Alan. 1954. "Linguistic Class-indicators in Present-day English." *Neuphilologische Mitteilungen* 55: 20–56.

Ross, Alan. 1959. "U and non-U. An Essay in Sociological Linguistics." In *Noblesse Oblige*, edited by Nancy Mitford, 11–20. Oxford: Oxford University Press.

Samuelson, Kate. 2016. "How *The Crown* Uses Real History to Make Drama." *Time*, November 4, 2016. https://time.com/4542526/the-crown-netflix-queen-elizabeth-history/.

Sandrelli, Annalisa. 2016. "*Downton Abbey* in Italian: Not Quite the Same." *Status Quaestionis* 11: 152–192. https://doi.org/10.13133/2239-1983/13836.

Santipolo, Matteo. 2006. *Le Varietà dell'Inglese Contemporaneo*. Roma: Carocci.

Savage, Mike, and Karel Williams, eds. 2008. *Remembering Elites*. Oxford: Blackwell.

Savage, Mike, Fiona Devine, Niall Cunningham, Mark Taylor, Yaojun Li, Johs. Hjellbrekke, Brigitte Le Roux, Sam Friedman, and Andrew Miles. 2016. "A New Model of Social Class? Findings from the BBC's Great British Class Survey Experiment." *Sociology* 47(2): 219–250.

Schegloff, Emanuel A., Gail Jefferson, and Harvey Sacks. 1977. "The Preference for Self-Correction in the Organization of Repair in Conversation." *Language* 53 (2): 361–382.

Schegloff, Emanuel A. 2000. "When 'Others' Initiate Repair." *Applied Linguistics* 21 (2): 205–243.

Schmid, Christina. 1999. "Estuary English: A Sociophonological Description Into a New Accent in the Southeast of England." MA diss., University of Vienna.

Seddon, Sean. 2016. "Made in Carlisle – But Dubbed into Geordie. News & Star." *News & Star*, August, 19, 2016. https://www.newsandstar.co.uk/news/16760212.made-in-carlisle-but-dubbed-into-geordie/.

Sidnell, Jack, ed. 2009. *Conversation Analysis: Comparative Perspectives*. Cambridge: Cambridge University Press.

Sidnell, Jack. 2016. "Conversation Analysis." *Oxford Research Encyclopaedias*, March 3, 2016.

Smith, Ben T. 2011. "Sign of the Times: William and Kate's Accents." *Dialect Blog*, May 1, 2011. http://dialectblog.com/2011/05/01/william-and-kates-accent/.

Sternberg, Meir. 1981. "Polylingualism as Reality and Translation as Mimesis." *Poetics Today* 2.4: 221–239.

Sturiale, Massimo. 2002. "RP: Received or Reference Pronunciation?" *Linguistica e Filologia*. 15: 89–112.

Taggart, Caroline. 2010. *Her Ladyship's Guide to the Queen's English*. London: National Trust.

Thomas, Erik R. 2013. "Sociophonetics." In *The Handbook of Language Variation and Change*, edited by Jack K. Chambers and Natalie Schilling, 108–122. Oxford: John Wiley & Sons.

Tieken-Boon van Ostade, Ingrid. 2009. *An Introduction to Late Modern English*. Edinburgh: Edinburgh University Press.

Trousdale, Graeme. 2010. *An Introduction to English Sociolinguistics*. Edinburgh: Edinburgh University Press.

Trudgill, Peter. 1972. "Sex, Covert Prestige and Linguistic Change in the Urban British English of Norwich." *Language in Society* 1: 179–195.

Trudgill, Peter. 1994. *Dialects*. London/New York: Routledge.

Trudgill, Peter. 1999. *The Dialects of England*. Oxford: Blackwell.

Trudgill, Peter. 2000. *Sociolinguistics: An Introduction to Language and Society*. London: Penguin.

Trudgill, Peter. 2003. *A Glossary of Sociolinguistics*. Edinburgh: Edinburgh University Press.

Trudgill, Peter. 2006. "Standard and Dialect Vocabulary." In *Encyclopedia of Language and Linguistics*, edited by Keith Brown, 119–121. Oxford: Elsevier.

Trudgill, Peter. 2008. "The Historical Sociolinguistics of Elite Accent Change: On Why RP is Not Disappearing." *Studia Anglica Posnaniesia* 44: 1–9.

"Uneasy Lies the Head of Production: Does it Matter if *The Crown* Fictionalises Reality?" *The Economist,* December 3, 2020. https://www.economist.com/leaders/2020/12/05/does-it-matter-if-the-crown-fictionalises-reality.

Upton, Clive. 2004. "Received Pronunciation." In *A Handbook of Varieties of English*, Volume 1: Phonology, edited by Edgar Schneider and Clive Upton, 217–230. Berlin: Mouton de Gruyter.

Valleriani, Luca. 2019. "Translating Regionalised Upper-Class English: Analysis of *The Prime of Miss Jean Brody* (1969)." Conference Paper Presentation at *Media For All 8 – Complex Understandings*, Stockholm University, June 17–19, 2019. https://www.tolk.su.se/english/media-for-all-8/programme/abstracts/translating-regionalised-upper-class-english-1.428547.

Valleriani, Luca. 2021a. " 'Why is He Making That Funny Noise?': The RP Speaker as an Outcast." In *The Dialects of British English in Fictional*

Texts, edited by Donatella Montini and Irene Ranzato 194-210. London/ New York: Routledge.

Valleriani, Luca. 2021b (forthcoming). "Upper-class English in *The Crown*: An Analysis of Dubbing and Subtitling." In *Recent Trends in Translation Studies: An Anglo-Italian Perspective*, edited by Sara Laviosa, Giovanni Iamartino, and Eileen Mulligan. Newcastle-upon-Tyne: Cambridge Scholars Publishing.

Wagg, Stephen. 1998. "'At Ease Corporal': Situation Comedy in British TV, from the 1950s to the 1990s." In *Because I Tell a Joke or Two: Comedy, Politics and Social Difference*, edited by Stephen Wagg, 1–31. London: Routledge.

Wales, Katie. 1994. "Royalese: The Rise and Fall of 'The Queen's English." *English Today* 39. 10 (3): 3–10.

Waugh, Evelyn. 1959. "An Open Letter to the Honourable Mrs. Peter Rodd on a Very Serious Subject." In *Noblesse Oblige*, edited by Nancy Mitford, 93–122. Oxford: Oxford University Press.

Wells, John C. 1992. *Accents of English 2. The British Isles.* Cambridge: Cambridge University Press.

Wells, John C. 1994. "The Cockneyfication of RP?" In *Nonstandard Varieties of Language. Stockholm Symposium*, Stockholm Studies in English LXXXIV, 198–205. Stockholm: Almqvist & Wiksell International.

Wells, John C. 1997a. "Is RP Turning Into Cockney?" In *Studies in Communicative Phonetics and Foreign Language Teaching Methodology*, edited by Margarita P. Dvorzhetska and A.A. Kalita, 10–15. Kyiv: State Linguistic University.

Wells, John C. 1997b. "Whatever Happened to Received Pronunciation?" *Jornadas de Estudios Ingleses* 2: 19–28.

Wells, John C. 1998. *Accents of English 1. An Introduction.* Cambridge: Cambridge University Press.

Windsor Lewis, Jack. 1972. *A Concise Pronouncing Dictionary of British and American English.* London: Oxford university Press.

Zabalbeascoa, Patrick. 2021 (196-199). "Some Observation on British Accent Stereotypes in Hollywood-style Films." In *The Dialects of British English in Fictional Texts*, edited by Donatella Montini and Irene Ranzato. London/ New York: Routledge.

Filmography

- Documentaries:
  BBC Royal Family. 1969. Richard Cawston. UK.
  BBC Monarchy: The Royal Family at Work. 2007. Matt Reid. UK.
  BBC Nancy Mitford: A Portrait by Her Sisters. 1980. Julian Jebb. UK.
  BBC The Coronation. 2018. Harvey Lilley. UK.

- Feature Films:
  Charlie and the Chocolate Factory. 2005. Tim Burton. USA/ UK.
  East is East. 1999. Daniel O'Donnell. UK.
  Educating Rita. 1983. Lewis Gilbert. UK.
  Emma. 2020. Autumn de Wilde. UK.
  The Favourite. 2018. Yorgos Lanthimos. Ireland/ UK/ USA.
  A Fish Called Wanda. 1988. Charles Chricton. UK.
  Four Weddings and a Funeral. 1994. Mike Newell. UK.
  Gosford Park. 2001. Robert Altman. UK.
  The Grass is Greener. 1960. Stanley Donen. UK.
  Hamilton (Disney+ streaming version). 2015. Lin-Manuel Miranda. USA.
  Harry Potter 5, 6, 7.1, 7.2. 2007–2011. David Yates. UK.
  Howards End. 1992. James Ivory. UK.
  The King's Speech. 2010. Tom Hooper. UK.
  The Lion King. 1994. Roger Allers and Rob Minkoff. USA.
  Mickey Blue Eyes. 1999. Kelly Makin. UK/ USA.
  The Prime of Miss Jean Brodie. 1969. Ronald Neame. UK.
  The Queen. 2006. Stephen Frears. UK.
  The Remains of the Day. 1993. James Ivory. USA/ UK.
  A Room with a View. 1985. James Ivory. UK.
  Upstairs Downstairs. 1971. Jean Marsh, Eileen Aitkins, John Hawkesworth and John Whitney. UK.

- TV series:
  Call the Midwife. 2012–present. Heidi Thomas. UK.
  The Crown. 2016–present. Peter Morgan. UK.
  Downton Abbey. 2010–2015. Julian Fellowes. UK/ USA.

The Fresh Prince of Bel Air. 1990–1996. Benny Medina and Jeff
    Pollack. USA.
Glee. 2009–2015. Ryan Murphy, Brad Falchuk and Ian Brennan. USA.
Peppa Pig. 2004–present. Neville Astley and Mark Baker. UK.
Upstairs Downstairs. 2010–2012. Heidi Thomas. UK.

Index of Names

ŁÓDŹ STUDIES IN LANGUAGE

Edited by

Barbara Lewandowska-Tomaszczyk and Łukasz Bogucki

www.peterlang.com